UNSEEN EUROPE A SURVEY OF EU POLITICS AND ITS IMPACT ON SPATIAL DEVELOPMENT IN THE NETHERLANDS

Nico van Ravesteyn
David Evers

NAi Publishers, Rotterdam
Netherlands Institute for Spatial Research, The Hague
2004

CONTENTS

Summary 7

Introduction
Justification and relevance of the research 11
Methods 12
Plan of the book 14

Context
The EU: establishment by evolution 17
Institutionalisation of European spatial
   planning 18
Constitutional Convention 22
Enlargement 23
Conclusions 25

Regional Policy
Introduction 29
EU policy 29
Consequences for the Netherlands 32
Conclusions 41

Transport
Introduction 45
EU policy 45
Consequences for the Netherlands 52
Conclusions 54

Agriculture
Introduction 59
EU policy 59
Consequences for the Netherlands 61
Conclusions 67

Competition Policy
Introduction 73
EU policy 73
Consequences for the Netherlands 76
Conclusions 82

Environment and Nature
Introduction 85
EU policy 85
Consequences for the Netherlands 87
Conclusions 97

Water
Introduction 101
EU policy 101
Consequences for the Netherlands 110
Conclusions 113

Spatial Policy Issues and the EU
Urban development policy 117
Rural areas policy 121
Mainports policy 126
Conclusions 132

Conclusions
Findings 137
Implications 140
Recommendations for further research 145

Literature 149

List of interviewees 156

About the authors 157

SUMMARY

The EU is involved, either directly or indirectly, in the most vital issues of national spatial policy.
— The indirect — and therefore usually unseen — consequences are often more significant, and will become increasingly so in the future.
— Although it certainly remains necessary to conduct spatial policy at the national level — if for no other reason than to coordinate EU sectoral policies and integrate them into the planning system — doing so without regard to the growing influence of Brussels will doom it to failure.
— Those involved in spatial policy should keep abreast of developments to avoid being caught off-guard by new EU directives or initiatives. The integration of EU sectoral policies in Dutch spatial planning is essential. At the moment, EU regulations continue to be implemented via the national sectors rather than via the spatial planning system.

Justification

Decisions on land use in the Netherlands are determined to a certain extent in Brussels. This is because, like all other Member States, the Netherlands has pledged to implement European legislation and directives in a complete, accurate, binding and timely fashion and because many of these European rules affect spatial developments. Examples include the preservation of natural habitats, caps on state aid and the various investments via EU agriculture, transport and regional policies. Despite these many impacts, the broader influence of EU policy on spatial developments in the Netherlands has still not been sufficiently investigated. This study addresses this by surveying a selected number of spatially relevant EU policy fields — i.e. regional policy, transport, agriculture, competition policy, environment and nature, and water — and their potential impacts in the Netherlands. This was done through a literature study and expert interviews. Besides the rather narrow goal of illustrating the EU's influence on Dutch spatial development, this survey can also be used to inform policymaking, and act as a springboard for further in-depth research.

Findings

Our survey found that for each EU policy field researched both direct and indirect spatial consequences were apparent in the Netherlands. The consequences of EU nature policy (Habitats and Birds Directives) are already obvious and considerable while the spatial effects of EU environmental and water policy will become more significant as time passes. Interestingly, however, the indirect consequences are often more significant, and will become increasingly so in the future. Taking regional policy as an example, the physical manifestations of EU investments are rather modest, especially if one takes the view that many of these projects may have proceeded without EU aid. However, the more unseen effects of these policies – especially in terms new administrative relationships – can ultimately be far greater. Also interesting in this respect are the potentially far-reaching land use implications of the production subsidies provided by the common agricultural policy, which have transformed the Dutch countryside over the past decades. By inference, the reform of these policies will have a great effect as well. By changing the rules of the game, vast tracts of land in the west of the Netherlands will be exposed to increased urban pressure, further eroding support for national planning policies based on urban concentration.

Similarly the mainports strategy – one of the cornerstones of Netherlands spatial planning policy since the 1980s – has in certain instances been rendered irrelevant by sweeping changes at the European level. The Single Sky and the liberalisation of the aviation industry have profound ramifications for the future of Schiphol, the regional business climate and the Dutch economy. Improved waterway connections on the European continent promoted via the TENs, also 'unseen' in the Netherlands, provide new opportunities for the Port of Rotterdam to maintain or enhance its position in the logistical chain of an enlarged Europe. And while the obligation on Member States to research or map out certain environmental conditions may seem rather benign, these can easily over time be translated into concrete agreements on minimum standards (e.g. Water Framework Directive) or at the very least be published as benchmarks, drawing negative attention to the countries who fare the worst.

Sectors and space

The Dutch government is often criticised for its sectoral approach, but this study has shown that the European policy framework is even more sectoral. It is therefore important for those involved in spatial policy to keep abreast of developments to avoid being caught off-guard by new directives or initiatives. At the same time, a more sectoral orientation can allow actors, such as Dutch planners, to align themselves with important policy areas at the EU level and gain more influence. In this context, it should be pointed out that the EU has a different sectoral organisation than the Netherlands. Even more important is the integration of EU sectoral policies in Dutch spatial planning. At the moment, EU regulations continue to be implemented via the national sectors rather than via the extensive spatial planning system.

Different cultures of enforcement

In the Netherlands, spatial issues are often resolved in a process of consensus building, involving lengthy consultation procedures and ad-hoc decision making. At the EU level, in contrast, rules are backed up with clear standards and performance indicators, and strict time schedules and monitoring requirements allow the European Commission to keep an eye on implementation. The difference in cultures between the Dutch and European way of dealing with rules can lead to conflict; the EU does not understand

Dutch tolerance. On the other hand, the emphasis placed by Europe on actual implementation and enforcement also has a positive effect; it gives citizens and civil organisations more certainty in their dealings with the government.

Coherence between Dutch and EU policy

Besides looking at the areas in which the Dutch and EU policies meet of conflict, it is also interesting to note where the two converge or diverge. The policies meet in the area of liberalisation and agricultural reform. Water, environmental and nature policy, though, are a different matter. Another interesting case of recent policy divergence is transport.

Conclusion

All in all, in the past decade, the new institutional context posed by the EU has fundamentally changed the relationship between Member States and their territory, despite the lack of a formal European competency to engage in spatial planning. Although it certainly remains necessary to conduct spatial policy at the national level – if for no other reason than to coordinate EU sectoral policies and integrate them into the planning system – doing so without regard to the growing influence of Brussels will doom it to failure.

INTRODUCTION

Justification and relevance of the research

Although vehemently denied in some circles, decisions on land use in the Netherlands are determined to a certain extent in Brussels. This is because, like all other Member States, the Netherlands has pledged to implement European legislation and directives in a complete, accurate, binding and timely fashion (Klinge-van Rooij et al. 2003: XVIII-XIX) and because many of these European rules have direct or indirect impacts on spatial development in the Netherlands. Numerous examples of this were reported in Dutch newspapers during the summer of 2003: EU air quality standards frustrating residential building plans; expansion of the Westerschelde Container Terminal on a derelict stretch of coastal land being held back by an EU habitat designation; Dutch citizens profiting from their right to free settlement by purchasing houses just over the German border. Perhaps the biggest story of all was about the fundamental changes now underway, and expected, as a result of the reform of EU agricultural policy. In addition to these examples are the less visible, but by no means less important, effects of EU policy: the introduction and impact of the European concepts of sustainability and subsidiarity in the Netherlands; the new alliances (e.g. PPP constructions, EU lobbying and cross-border cooperation); and the many new opportunities and threats that EU enlargement will bring (e.g. in economic markets, transport and logistics).

Despite these many impacts, the broader influence of EU policy on spatial developments in the Netherlands has not yet been investigated. Various organisations have studied single policy areas, such as the Structural Funds (ERAC 2003; Ecorys 2003) or the TENs policy (Hajer 2000). There is also a rich and growing literature on the genesis of spatial policy at the European level, of which the 1999 ESDP is the best known product (Faludi and Waterhout 2002). Faludi and Zonneveld (1998a) carried out an extensive study on the effect of EU policy on Dutch spatial planning policy, but this stopped short of examining actual spatial developments, and has already become dated in the fast-moving world of EU policy.

This study attempts to fill a perceived gap in the literature by surveying spatially relevant EU policy fields and their impacts in the Netherlands. Our hypothesis is that spatial developments in the Netherlands are influenced to an important degree by EU policy. To investigate this, we selected a number of spatially relevant sectoral policy areas at the EU level (there is no institutionalised spatial planning as such at the EU level) and examined their potential impacts by studying the literature and interviewing experts. Because we focused on spatial developments rather than spatial policy, we investigated some activities of the European Union that are often excluded from planning studies (e.g. competition policy and agriculture). Besides the rather narrow goal of illustrating the EU's influence on Dutch spatial development, this survey provides a springboard for further in-depth research and can be used to inform policymaking. For this reason, we indicate whether a particular issue is fruitful for further research and what lessons our findings may have for Dutch policy.

The EU is often – undeservedly – portrayed as dull, esoteric, opaque and remote. We hope that this survey may also raise the level of awareness of and appreciation for the EU among researchers and policymakers by collating a great deal of relevant material for further reflection. We found a wealth of information readily available from EU sources in a variety of languages, usually directly accessible from the main website (www.europa.eu.int), and the EU representatives were eager to lend assistance and offer additional information.

In short, the aim of this study is twofold: to take stock of how the EU affects spatial developments in the Netherlands, and to raise the general level of awareness for the EU among researchers in urban and regional planning, policymakers and civil servants.

Methods

There are various avenues through which EU policy can affect spatial developments. Figure 1 provides a general illustration of how the use of space can be directly and indirectly affected, and shows the position of the EU in this change. In this view, socioeconomic developments create different pressures for land use that are often, but not always, mediated (e.g. amplified, diverted or mitigated) by regulations, planning systems or legislation. The result is a change in the way land is used, valued or traversed.

Whereas much attention has been paid to the evolution of EU spatial policy and its effect on planning policy in the Member States (Faludi and Zonneveld 1998a; Tewdwr-Jones and Williams 2001), this study investigates the effect of EU policy on actual spatial developments, either directly (right-hand arrow in Figure 1) or indirectly via the Member State and/or its planning system. To aid our investigation, we have further operationalised this distinction between direct and indirect impacts.

Direct impacts
Broadly speaking, EU policy and legislation can have direct impacts on spatial developments through measures employed to facilitate development, such as providing information and subsidies (carrots) or through measures that restrict developmental options (sticks). We can attempt to quantify this impact by considering a number of different dimensions:
– physical size of the affected area (m^2/ha)
– size of area-based investment (€)
– reprioritisation of projects (time).
In our investigation we always looked for these characteristics of the size, cost and timing of spatial developments, but did not always find them. We used

Figure 1. Direct and indirect influences of the EU on spatial developments

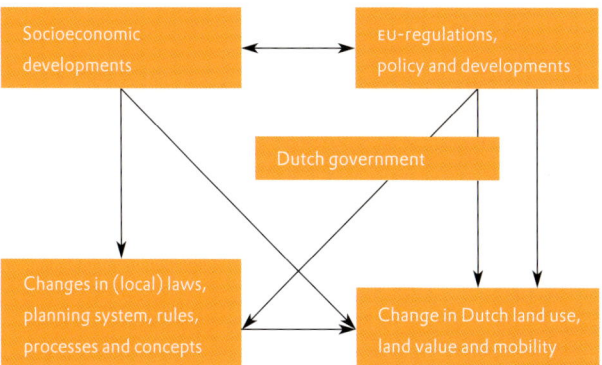

existing data when available, but did not generate new data ourselves owing to the wide scope of our survey (topic and scale). It might be possible to do this in a follow-up study limited to an in-depth analysis or case study of one or more locations; but even then, the practice of co-financing can complicate the extent to which a particular development can be ascribed to the EU.

Indirect impacts
Even more difficult to quantify, but no less important, are the ways in which the EU indirectly affects spatial developments. Where EU rules are incorporated into national legislation it becomes difficult to state with confidence whether subsequent developments were a result of EU policy or national policy; in some cases, the Member State would have introduced the same kind of legislation anyway. The EU can influence spatial developments indirectly in a number of ways, by:
– introducing new spatial concepts (e.g. sustainable development)
– creating new administrative relationships (e.g. EU/region, Interreg)
– redrawing mental maps (especially in border areas)
– creating new economic activity (e.g. via the internal market or new infrastructure links)
– providing information (e.g. publishing rankings of Member States or providing sound spatial data (ESPON) can affect policy decisions).

Obviously, establishing a scientifically valid cause–effect relationship was not feasible within the context of this brief survey; this requires more in-depth research. For this reason, the link between policy (cause) and spatial development (effect), as well as statements about future developments, are based entirely on opinions found within the relevant literature and on our discussions with experts. At the end of the survey, we discuss what would be needed for a follow-up study to more adequately demonstrate the link between EU policy and Dutch spatial developments.

Plan of book

In the next chapter we will provide an overview of the most important institutional characteristics of the European Union and some of the most salient developments and challenges currently facing it. The following six chapters will then take a closer look at how sectoral EU policies affect spatial developments in the Netherlands. Each of the substantive chapters focuses on a single policy area: regions, transport, agriculture, competition, environment and water. The chapter on 'Spatial policy issues and the EU' reverses the perspective taken in the previous chapters by examining three major spatial policy issues facing the Netherlands today (urbanisation, rural development and mainports), and exposing the largely unseen effects of EU policy. In the last chapter we present a summary of our findings and reflect on the implications this has for Dutch spatial planning. Finally, as this survey is intended as a springboard for further investigation, we provide an overview of the topics we studied in terms of their potential for in-depth research.

Context

CONTEXT

The purpose of this chapter is to provide a background for understanding the spatial impact of specific EU policy areas. It contains an overview of the European Union and some of the most important developments facing Europe today. The topics discussed here will have a wide array of consequences in the different policy contexts and will be revisited where appropriate in the following chapters.

The EU: establishment by evolution

Unlike most world powers, the origins of the European Union – now on the brink of ratifying a constitution and a historic ten-nation expansion – are rather modest. It began with a treaty between six nations on steel and coal in the early 1950s. In 1957, these countries signed a landmark treaty on free trade in Rome (EEC), which was to lay the groundwork for fifty years of unbroken and intensifying economic cooperation. Over time, the liberalisation of trade grew into a larger common market, culminating in the introduction of a single currency in several Member States. At the same time, other kinds of decisions were made and policy was formulated at the EU level, usually to create a level playing field for fair competition, or to deal with transnational matters, such as the natural environment or fisheries. Since then, the competences of the EU have expanded to include traditionally national policy areas such as transport, competition, regional economic development and agriculture. As a reflection of these ambitions, the EU budget has grown tremendously since the 1960s, from a virtually negligible level to almost 96 billion Euros in 2002 – approximately equal to the GDP of a smaller Member State (ERAC 2003: 34).

A number of institutions have been founded to coordinate the various areas in which the EU acts. At present, there is the directly elected Parliament, the Council (in which Member States are represented) and the twenty-member European Commission. The latter is the closest thing to an executive government at the EU level and has been called 'the powerhouse of European integration' (Faludi and Waterhout 2002).

The rules and resource allocations determined at the EU level are having an increasing effect on policymaking in the Member States and are directly or indirectly changing the course of land use and urban development. Until recently, these effects were a product of policy emanating from various departments, but growing interest in European spatial planning may very well lead to a new echelon of planning in Europe. This is the subject of the next section.

Institutionalisation of European spatial planning

The European Union is authorised to act in a variety of policy areas, but spatial planning is not one of them: there is no formal system of spatial planning at the European level. One of the reasons for this is that intervention in this area could be construed by Member States as an encroachment on the sovereignty over their own territories and an infringement of the subsidiarity principle. On the other hand, as this study will show clearly for the Netherlands, the EU has not been unwilling to conduct spatially relevant policy through its sectoral competences, usually arguing that establishing a level playing field for competition, addressing Communitywide problems and dealing with cross-border problems justifies intervention.

European Spatial Development Perspective (ESDP)
It may seem odd that the EU has the formal powers to conduct policies with a spatial impact, but is not authorised to develop a spatial framework to coordinate them (for more on this see Robert et al, 2001; Buunk 2003). To redress this imbalance, various informal steps have been taken (meetings between planning ministers of the Member States) to draw up a strategy for spatial development at the European level. The various discussions, studies and maps produced during this ten-year process led to the adoption of the European Spatial Development Perspective (ESDP) at an informal conference of planning ministers in Potsdam in 1999. This informal document is the closest the EU has come to a comprehensive and integral statement on spatial developments in the European territory. Although it has no formal status as a plan or policy document, the ESDP was formulated in a collaborative manner between planning representatives from the Member States, and thus enjoys wide political support in the European planning community (Faludi and Waterhout 2002; Faludi 2002). The three main principles of the ESDP are (cf. Figure 3):
  – development of a balanced and polycentric urban system and a new urban-rural relationship;
  – securing parity of access to infrastructure and knowledge;
  – sustainable development, prudent management and protection of nature and the cultural heritage.

Although these three main principles leave much room for interpretation, especially in how they are to be achieved, they do represent to a large degree many of the goals articulated by the different Commission departments. It should also be pointed out that these goals are not altogether harmonious; it is easy to argue, for example, that parity of access to infrastructure may conflict with environmental interests (Richardson and Jensen 2000).

Despite its lack of a formal status, the ESDP is already being used in a variety of ways. An action programme drawn up in 1999 to increase the influence of this document includes items such as incorporating it in geography textbooks for use in secondary schools, introducing territorial impact assessments, establishing a 'Future Regions of Europe' award and, more importantly,

Figure 2. Milestones in European integration

						1985	1990	1993	2000
1952						Single	first	Single market	Lisbon strategy
European Coal and						European	stage	1994	2001
Steel Community						Act	of EMU	second stage	Introduction of Euro
(1951 Treaty of Paris)								of EMU	as currency

		1973		1981	1986		1995	2004 (May)
		UK, IRL, DK		Greece	Spain and Portugal		S, FIN, A	10 states

1989   1994 Leipzig principles
Start of   1997 First draft ESDP (Noordwijk)
ESDP process   1999 ESDP (Potsdam)
in Nantes   2000 ESPON

1992   2001
Rio Convention   Environment 2010
on sustainable   (Sixth Environmental
development   action plan)

Habitat directive

1992   Agenda 2000
Agriculture   reform of agricultural
policy reform   policy

1996 TEN-T Essen priority projects
2001 TEN-T update
2003 TEN-T
Quick Start

1950	1960	1970	1980	1990	2000	
Genesis				**Breakthrough**	**Consolidation**	**Institutionalization**

1949
Council
of Europe

1979   1985   1991   1997
Direct   Assembly   Charter of   Treaty of
election   of European   the regions   Amsterdam
Euro   Regions   of the community
Parliament
                                      Eurocities
                                      1992
                                      EU
                                      (Maastricht Treaty)

1958   1986   1993   2004
– EEC   – Single   – European Union   – EU constitution
  (1957 Treaty of Rome)   European   – Common foreign   – Territorial Cohesion
– Council of Ministers   Act   and security policy – ESDP-2?
– Commission   – Art. 130   – EU Citizenship
– European Parliament   on economic   – Committee of
– European Court of Justice   and social   the regions
– Economic and Social   cohesion   – Subsidiarity
  Committee   principle

1965	1969	1975	1979	1984	1989	1993	1999	2004
First	Second	European	First	Second	Third	Fourth	Fifth	Sixth
commu-	communi-	Regional	reform	reform	reform	reform	reform	reform
nication	cation	Develop-	structural	structural	struc-	structural	structural	structural
on	on regional	ment	funds	funds	tural	funds	funds	funds
regional	policy	Fund			funds			
policy								

Context   18 · 19

Figure 3. Convergence of ESDP principles

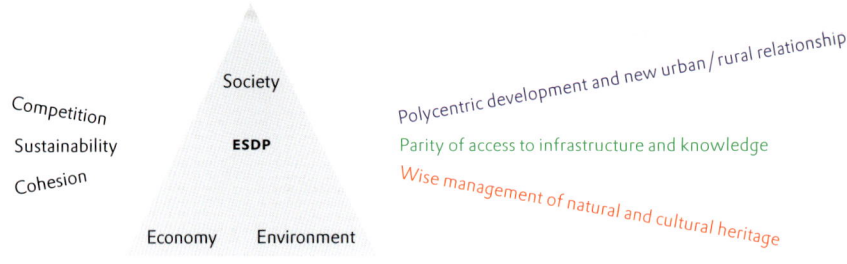

Source: Ministerie van VROM (1999)

funding various interregional (Interreg) projects (Faludi and Waterhout 2002: 161). It has even found its way into some official policy documents and statements. Examples include the *Second Report on Economic and Social Cohesion*, the latest annual report on Structural Funds implementation, the *Sixth Community Environmental Programme*, a Recommendation on Integrated Coastal Zone Management and, perhaps most importantly, the 2001 White Paper *European Governance*, which singled out the intention of the Commission to build on the ESDP in its sustainable development strategy (Faludi and Waterhout 2002: 174-5).

European Spatial Planning Observation Network (ESPON)
For planners, one of the most interesting products of the ESDP process is the network of spatial planning observatories, ESPON, established at the 1999 Potsdam meeting. Its mission is to formulate dependable criteria and indicators for the establishment of typologies of regions and urban areas.[1] Examples include traffic flows and accessibility, economic cooperation, urban networks, and risks of natural disasters. This comprehensive spatial survey will also enable long-term research to be carried out on spatial issues at the EU level. Besides the political impact such research may have, ESPON also supplies the technical and scientific knowledge needed to implement the policy options in the ESDP and translate them into appropriate legal and financial instruments (Committee on Spatial Development 1999: 91–92). In addition, by providing comparable data for all the Member States, the candidate countries, Norway and Switzerland, ESPON can become a very interesting and potentially valuable source of material for further comparative or regional research (benchmarking). Pan-European ESPON data and cartographic information will also prove invaluable in updating the ESDP, if Europe decides to embark on this.

ESPON's tasks, priorities and working methods are meticulously described in the ESPON 2006 Programme (final version 30 January 2002, www.espon.lu). This rather broad programme (see below) began with vigour and has already produced some noteworthy interim reports. The final reports are due in August 2004.

1. As its name implies, ESPON refers to a network of organisations rather than a new EU institution. It is based in Luxemburg and headed by the Committee for Spatial Development (a committee consisting of one high-ranking official from each Member State in the area of spatial and regional policy) and a Monitoring Committee. The group of ESPON contact points (one for each Member State) takes care of the actual implementation of the programme. ESPON is funded through the EU Interreg III Programme, also partly a product of the ESDP. A sum of €12 million has been reserved for the required research in the 2002–2006 period (50% of which is financed by the EU and 50% by the Member States involved).

Table 1. The ESPON 2006 Programme

Priority 1	**Thematic projects on important spatial developments**
Measure 1.1	Cities, polycentric development and urban–rural relations
1.1.1	The role, specific situation and potentials of urban areas as nodes of a polycentric development
1.1.2	Urban–rural relations
1.1.3	Particular effects of enlargement and beyond for the polycentric spatial tissue
1.1.4	The spatial effects of demographic trends and migration
Measure 1.2	Parity of access to infrastructure and knowledge
1.2.1	Basic supply of infrastructure for territorial cohesion
1.2.2	Spatial effects of networks, transport and (tele)communication services
1.2.3	Identification of spatially relevant aspects of the information society
Measure 1.3	Natural and cultural heritage
1.3.1	The spatial effects and management of natural and technological hazards in general and in relation to climate change
1.3.2	Management of the natural heritage
1.3.3	The role and spatial effects of cultural heritage and identity
Priority 2	**Policy impact projects**
Measure 2.1	The territorial effects of sector policies
2.1.1	Spatial diversification by the infrastructure policy of TENs
2.1.2	Spatial effects of the EU R&D policy
2.1.3	Spatial effects of the EU Agricultural Policy with particular reference to the environmental dimension and policy
Measure 2.2	New territorial aspects of the Structural Funds and related Funds
2.2.1	The territorial effects of the Structural Funds, pre-accession aid and Phare/Tacis/ISPA
2.2.2	The effects of Structural Funds in urban areas
Measure 2.3	Institutions and instruments of spatial policies
2.3.1	The application and effects of the ESDP in the Member States
2.3.2	The coordination of territorial and urban oriented policy from EU to the local level
Priority 3	**Coordinating cross-thematic projects**
Measure 3.1	Integrated tools for the European spatial development
Measure 3.2	Spatial scenarios and orientations towards the ESDP and the Cohesion Policy

Source: ESPON Programme, version 30 January 2002

In addition to ESPON, the EU also finances some spatially relevant research through its Framework Programmes.[2] This supports the EU's aim, articulated at the Lisbon summit in 2000, of becoming the most competitive and dynamic knowledge economy in the world by 2010.[3] The results of the research conducted under the Fifth Framework Programme are now becoming available, the most spatially interesting being those on 'competitive and sustainable growth' and 'energy, environment and sustainable development'. The most relevant topic for spatial research in the current programme is 'global change and ecosystems', which has a budget of about 700 million Euros.

Despite the existence of the ESDP and ESPON, the future of European spatial planning remains uncertain. There is still no formal planning subject at the European level with the authority to impose its views on unwilling Member States; everything continues to be implemented on a voluntary basis. Moreover, the EU still lacks a legal basis for spatial planning, although as the next section will show, the inclusion of the term 'territorial cohesion' in the Draft Constitution may imply this. The enlargement of the EU will also make many of the conceptualisations of European space in the ESDP obsolete. Nevertheless, despite its non-binding status, the ESDP has been influential in several relevant sectoral policy areas (Ministerie van VROM 1999; Waterhout 2002). Its importance lies not so much in the document itself, but in the forging of new alliances in European spatial planning, the introduction and acceptance of common planning concepts in the long term, and the creation of 'an arena for a discourse on European space' (Faludi and Zonneveld 1998a: 263).

Constitutional Convention

The unveiling of the Draft Constitution in July 2003 signals a new era in European cooperation. If adopted by the Member States, this document will arguably become the greatest milestone in the EU's long development and cement its legitimacy as a tier of government. The creation of a constitution is seen as an essential precondition for the continued functioning of Europe after the enlargement. Although the content of the Draft Constitution continues to be debated at the EU level and in the current and future Member States (including referenda), it is expected that the main passages relevant to spatial policy will survive relatively unscathed. The stumbling blocks to the ratification encountered in late 2003 resulted primarily from disagreement over voting rights.

For spatial planners, the vital issue is what this document could mean for planning at the European level. Currently, planning is not an EU competence, nor is the current institutional arrangement of the EU equipped to handle it. This could change, however, with the inclusion of the concept of 'territorial cohesion' in several passages of the Draft Constitution. According to this document, one of the duties of the Union is to 'promote economic, social and territorial cohesion, and solidarity among Member States' (I-3-3). The draft further stipulates that the Union shares competence with the Member States in the principle area of 'economic, social and territorial cohesion' (I-13-2).

---

2. The Sixth Framework Programme is a subsidy instrument to stimulate scientific research in the EU. The aim is to promote a European Research Area and reduce the R&D gap with the United States and Japan through improved cooperation between European institutes. The total available budget is €17.5 billion for 2003–2006. As with many other EU programmes, Sixth Framework funds are issued according to the principle of co-financing: over half of the funds must come from other sources.

3. The strategy for achieving this includes a broad package of economic, social, environmental and research items. Further agreements have been made with national governments about such things as increasing R&D expenditures, improving education, the Single European Sky, the reduction of obstructive regulations for small and medium-sized enterprises and ICT networks, and the establishment of a European risk capital fund for ICT projects.

This shared competence also applies to the internal market, agriculture and fisheries, transport, energy and the environment, and means that both the EU and the Member States are authorised to act in a particular area. As in these other areas, when in doubt, the authority of the EU will take precedence as a higher tier of authority. On the other hand, this is kept in check by the subsidiarity principle which limits the range of activities the EU may undertake:

> Under the principle of subsidiarity, in areas which do not fall within its exclusive competence the Union shall act only if and insofar as the objectives of the intended action cannot be sufficiently achieved by the Member States, either at central level or at regional and local level, but can rather, by reason of the scale or effects of the proposed action, be better achieved at Union level. (1-9-3)

In short, spatial planning will remain a clear national activity as long as the EU does not infuse the term 'territorial cohesion' with a meaning that would enable the Union to act to promote it, and then chooses to act on this basis. Unfortunately, there is little agreement on how this rather vague concept will or should be interpreted, and it may be left to precedent to settle the issue.[4] If territorial cohesion does become an EU competence, it could provide the key to a future ESDP with binding force rather than voluntary adherence. The current document is already in need of an update due to the new stream of insights being provided by ESPON and, more importantly, the enlargement.

Enlargement

Probably the most fundamental change to the European Union in the near future will be the enlargement by ten Member States in May 2004 (cf. Figure 4). For many people this has come as somewhat of a surprise, but the processes that led to this decision have been in motion for over a decade. In 1993 the European Council, meeting in Copenhagen, agreed to establish political, economic and administrative criteria for entry into the Union; nine years later in the same city, the Council agreed on the largest expansion of the EU in its history. This enlargement is different from previous ones because all the accession countries, except the islands of Cyprus and Malta, are former communist countries in Central and Eastern Europe (i.e. Poland, Hungary, the Czech Republic, Slovakia, Slovenia, Latvia, Estonia and Lithuania). Negotiations with Romania and Bulgaria are already underway on their possible entry into the Union a few years later, which would bring the total number of EU Member States to twenty-seven, and Turkey has already expressed a keen interest in becoming the first Moslem EU Member State. The expansion, including Romania and Bulgaria, will increase the total landmass of the EU by 34 per cent and its population by approximately 105 million (CPB 2003: 24). Nevertheless, since the GDP per capita of the accession countries is only about 40 per cent of the EU average, their combined GDP is comparable to that of the Netherlands (de Mooij and Nahuis, 2003: 14). Unemployment is also higher, at about 15 per cent in 2000, which is roughly twice the EU average.

[4]. The formal designation of territorial cohesion as an EU competence could lead to a new model for coordination: the linking of sectoral (vertical) policy areas and instruments for (horizontal) coordination of those elements that have or could have territorial effects. This is how the concept of territorial cohesion was introduced in an influential commentary on the strict sectoral organisation of the European Commission (Robert et al. 2001).

Not surprisingly, much of the discourse surrounding the enlargement has centred on the *budgetary consequences* of the weak economic position of the ten new Member States. Following their accession, these countries will have the same rights and duties as other EU countries, including the right to agricultural and regional cohesion support. This has prompted calls for reform in both these policy areas. An unmodified *agricultural/rural areas policy* would require an additional 14.5 billion Euros (the budget is currently about €40 billion), which would be in direct violation of the 2002 Copenhagen agreement to limit increases in expenditure to 1 per cent each year (de Mooij and Nahuis 2003: 13). Similarly, an unmodified *Structural Funds policy* would require an annual increase in the budget of 7 billion Euros, or 20 per cent, which is politically unacceptable to various Member States (Ministerie van BZ 2001).[5] In all, the enlargement will have a profound impact on the future of the EU's two largest budgets, agriculture and regional cohesion.

Perhaps of greater importance to the future of Europe than such budgetary matters is the effect of the internal market. By eliminating trade barriers and standardising regulations throughout the enlarged Union, commerce between new and old Member States will grow rapidly. It is expected that the opening up of new markets and the introduction of foreign competition will result in an increase in scale of economic activities and specialisation. Interestingly, the relatively modern and efficient Dutch agricultural sector may stand to gain from the enlargement by supplying produce to candidate countries like Poland at a lower price than local producers can offer. Haulage and logistics companies will also profit from increased trade, while other sectors will probably suffer from the increased competition. On balance, the enlargement is expected to have a minor but positive impact on the Dutch economy. Another aspect of the internal market, the right of citizens to free movement, is expected to increase migration in the EU, although predictions of the number of migrants from new Member States vary widely (from 1 to 13 million). Generally it is expected that relatively few (1%) will settle in the Netherlands; unless one considers the possible accession of Turkey (de Mooij and Nahuis, 2003: 19; CPB 2003: 34–38).

It is important to note that changes in the economic structure of Europe can affect the spatial structure and demography as well. The enlargement of the EU with ten new Member States in 2004, and in all probability two more soon after, will have far-reaching implications for EU *spatial policy* (insofar it exists). Since the ESDP is the outcome of discussions between the fifteen Member States it will obviously be inadequate for a 25/27-member Union. The enlargement will alter the physical area of the EU, changing urban–rural relationships and creating new border regions. It will also have massive consequences for transport. Finally, the enlargement will bring with it new environmental and economic development challenges, which are discussed in detail in the Chapters on 'Environment and nature' and 'Regional Policy' respectively.

5. Since Southern European countries would stand to lose most of their funding, they may seek to lower the Objective 1 threshold in order to continue to receive aid. Other net contributors, the Netherlands included, may seek to reduce their contributions.s

Figure 4. Enlargement of the EU and GDP per capita, 2000

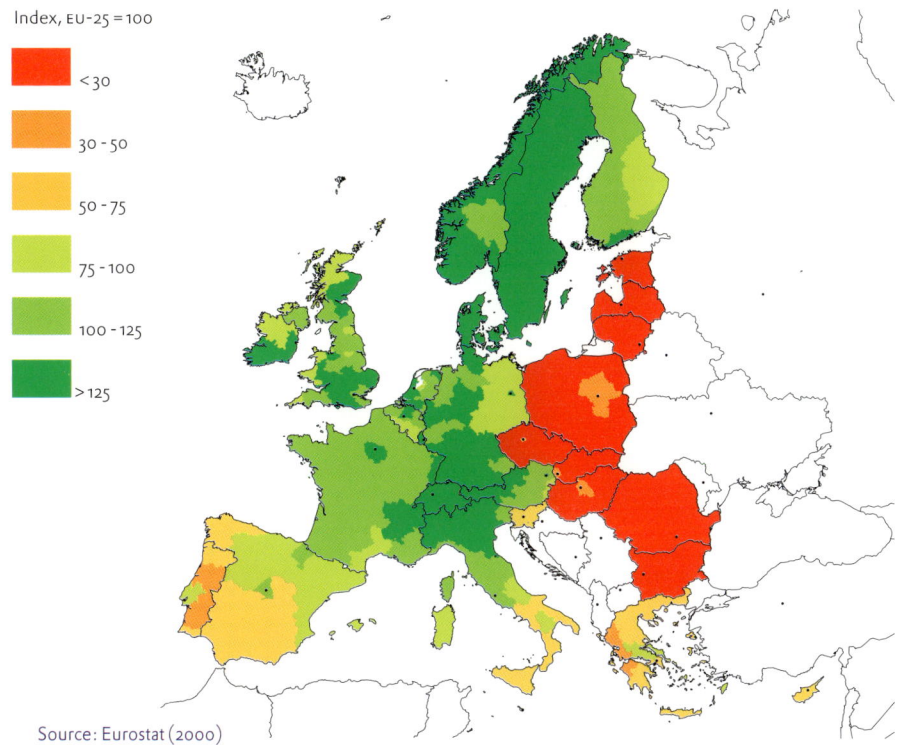

Source: Eurostat (2000)

Conclusions

The EU is an ever-changing construct, evolving from the one treaty to the other and continually finding new competences to legitimate its existence; including it would seem, spatial planning. At the same time, the EU is also an entity on the brink of an institutional rebirth: a new Constitution, a brave expansion eastwards, and the ambition to become the world's best knowledge-based economy. While so much seems uncertain and open, EU policy continues to resonate and affect spatial developments in the Member States in a variety of distinct ways. In some areas, the influence of Brussels will increase, while in others it will diminish. It is the task of this survey to take stock of the spatial impact of EU policy in the Netherlands, not just now, but in the light of the sweeping changes discussed in this chapter.

The following chapters will take a closer look at how sectoral EU policies affect spatial developments in the Netherlands. The topics chosen reflect those in the spatial planning literature (e.g. Committee on Spatial Development 1999; Robert et al. 2001; Tewdwr-Jones and Williams 2001; Vet and Reincke 2002) and fall more or less into the categories of 'carrots' and 'sticks': they attempt to effect change either by providing positive stimuli, such as subsidies and information, or by imposing restrictions (cf. van Schendelen 2002). Although a combination of both strategies is employed most of the time, the first three topics (regional policy, transport and agriculture) generally gravitate towards the 'carrot' approach, while the latter three topics (competition, environment and water) rely more on 'sticks' to bring about change. A third kind of policy instrument, persuasion via coordination and information ('name and shame'), is usually used in combination with the 'sticks' approach and is more prominent in later chapters.

Regional Policy

REGIONAL POLICY

Introduction

Although the European Union does not have the formal competence to engage in spatial planning, it is our conviction that its sectoral policies do have a clear impact on land use and development in the Member States. The most obvious example is the EU's regional policy which, under the banner of 'cohesion,' seeks to mitigate socioeconomic disparities between European regions. By channelling funds to projects such as roads, bridges and office parks, the physical impacts of EU regional policy are readily discernable. EU regional support in the form of 'place-based' subsidies and retraining programmes can also produce shifts in investments over space, although the effects of this cannot be observed directly.

In this chapter we first map out the basic framework of EU regional policy and its most important instrument, the Structural Funds, including an overview of the funding levels for the various programmes. We then examine how these funds have affected spatial developments and the way planning is done in the Netherlands. We conclude with a discussion on the changes to EU regional policy now underway and their ramifications for the Netherlands.

EU policy

In the early years of European cooperation, most of the participating countries had roughly the same level of national economic development, but there were greater disparities between the regions within them. To live up to its commitment of providing a level economic playing field, Europe embarked on a regional policy to reduce these disparities. As early as 1958, the European Social Fund (ESF) and European Agricultural Guidance and Guarantee Fund (EAGGF) were set up to soften the harsher effects of the common market. With the entrance of Britain to the European Community in 1973, the problem of economic restructuring became apparent, and the vastly important European Regional Development Fund (ERDF) was established to address this problem. Later, when Greece (1981), Spain and Portugal (1986) joined the EC, disparities in income levels were no longer restricted to regions within countries but also existed between Member States. The Cohesion Fund was set up to enable the new Member States to catch up. At the end of the 1980s, the various regional funds were reorganised and renamed the Structural Funds, which are administered according to a programme of roughly five years. The budget was also increased.

The first Structural Funds period (1989-1993) saw the inclusion of cohesion as one of the primary objectives of the European Union in the Maastricht Treaty, and a corresponding budgetary increase to ECU 68 billion (1997 prices). In the second Structural Funds period (1994–1999) the budget more than doubled to almost ECU 177 billion. The third and current Structural Funds period (2000–2006) has the largest budget to date. Regional policy now comprises over 35 per cent of the total EU budget and is second only to agriculture in terms of expenditure (Ederveen et al. 2002). Despite this phenomenal growth, the Structural Funds budget still is only about 0.45 per cent of total EU GDP (currently the total EU budget is around 1 per cent, with an official ceiling of 1.27% of total GDP). Table 2 provides an overview of the total expenditure on cohesion policy for the current period.

Table 2. Regional policy budget for the current period

EU Regional policy	Total budget for the 2000–2006 period (in 1999 euros)
Structural Funds	
– Objective 1	135.90 billion
– Objective 2	22.50 billion
– Objective 3	24.05 billion
Community Initiatives	10.44 billion
Fisheries	1.11 billion
Innovative actions	1.00 billion
Regional funds total	195.00 billion
Cohesion Fund	18.00 billion
Total regional policy	213.00 billion

Source: European Commission (2002c)

As Table 2 shows, the majority of EU funding (70%) is targeted at regions whose development is lagging behind (Objective 1), a further 11.5 per cent is earmarked for economic and social restructuring (Objective 2) and 12.3 per cent of the funding is directed at promoting the modernisation of training systems and job creation (Objective 3). In addition, the EU provides funding for the adjustment of fisheries outside Objective 1 regions (0.5%) and innovative actions to promote and experiment with new ideas on development (0.51%). Community Initiatives (5.35%) address specific problems, including:
 – cross-border, transnational and interregional cooperation (Interreg III)
 – sustainable development of cities and declining urban areas (Urban II)
 – rural development through local initiatives (Leader+)
 – combating inequality and discrimination in access to the labour market (Equal).

In addition to the Structural Funds, the Cohesion Fund provides direct finance for specific projects relating to environmental and transport infrastructure in Spain, Greece, Ireland and Portugal; the Instrument for Structural Policies for pre-Accession (ISPA) provides assistance along the same lines to the ten countries joining the EU in 2004.

Obtaining funding: the process

The allocation of EU funds is a complex process involving various tiers of government. According to the current process, the budget and goals for the upcoming period are set by the European Council. Member States can draw up programme proposals and submit them to the Commission for review. In the review process, the EU assesses proposals against a funding condition of additionality: applicants must argue that the project would have not been feasible or carried out without extra Community support. To ensure that the projects funded by EU money have merit or promise, the EU also requires that they are co-financed by thae public and/or (preferably in terms of leverage) the private sector. Together, these measures seek to ensure that EU support provides that critical 'push over the edge' to ensure that worthwhile projects are carried out. In the next stage, the programmes are discussed and implementation strategies and funding levels are designated. Deciding on the actual projects to be funded within the framework of the programmes is a matter for decentralised authorities and their partners. However, they are still monitored for compliance with EU objectives and effectiveness according to EU defined criteria.

Effects of regional policy in Europe

There is widespread disagreement about the effects of EU cohesion policy and the effectiveness of the Structural Funds in particular. Since the introduction of the regional policy, economic disparities between Member States have notably declined, yet they have remained about the same between regions, and actually increased within Member States (de Vet and Reincke 2002). This strange development leaves much room for interpretation. Although evaluations by the European Union have been (unsurprisingly) positive (e.g. European Commission 2001a: 30), there are some who argue that regional policy has had little or no effect (de Mooij and Tang 2002). Others are even more pessimistic, arguing that the Structural Funds work counterproductively. These authors claim that regions will eventually converge as a result of general economic development and that the cohesion policy, by dampening this through reallocation, can inhibit this natural cohesion process. Other arguments against the deployment of Structural Funds are that:
 – they crowd out private sector investments instead of stimulating them;
 – they reward Member States for neglecting regional disparities in their own countries;
 – the bureaucratic burden of the rules imposed in the allocation of funds dampens economic stimulation;
 – political manoeuvring has created a 'money go round' in which many funds circulate among wealthier Member States;
 – deploying regional funds for new infrastructure can lead to environmental damage and expose sensitive economies to fierce competition.

In short, the Structural Funds, stretched by attempts to obtain political support for the EU among the wealthier Member States, are accused of having become an unwieldy and ineffective instrument for achieving economic and social cohesion and potentially causing environmental damage – not to mention generally violating the subsidiarity principle.

Partly in response to this criticism, reform of the Structural Funds has been high on the European agenda. As indicated in the previous chapter, the discussions are also framed by several major institutional developments. The *enlargement* of the EU has raised fears among current Member States about the cost of an unmodified regional policy. After the enlargement, regional disparities in the EU will nearly double and a continuation of the Structural Funds under the current system would require a budget of approximately 360 billion Euros for the 2007–2013 period (Redeker 2002: 593). In this scenario, 'net-payers' like the Netherlands would find themselves obliged to contribute even more, whereas countries like Spain and Portugal would lose a substantial amount of the aid they enjoyed in previous Structural/Cohesion Fund programmes. Although not official policy, the *institutionalisation of European spatial planning* (the ESDP) has already affected the allocation of the Structural Funds by drawing attention to the importance of territorial coordination. Another issue concerns the implications of the inclusion of 'territorial cohesion' in the *Draft Constitution*: it remains to be seen which interpretation of this contested concept will prevail, but if it is endowed with sufficient meaning, it may serve as one of the guiding principles for the reform of the EU's regional policy. If the European Union really is determined to become the most dynamic and competitive knowledge-based region in the world, as agreed at the European Council *Lisbon summit* in March 2000, it may have to rethink some of its investment priorities, particularly the philosophy of channelling support to weaker regions rather than those with high economic potential. All these issues have made the future of the Structural Funds highly contentious.

A first statement by the Commission on regional policy in the 2007–2013 period was made in the long-awaited *Third Report on Economic and Social Cohesion*, published on 18 February 2004. Here, we can already see which forces seem to have prevailed in the latest rounds of negotiations. As expected, much of the attention of the report is devoted to ameliorating the disparities between current Member States and the accession countries. The most substantive change to the Structural Funds is the replacement of numbered Objectives with Community priorities. The priority 'convergence' resembles Objective 1 and is directed to the economic and social cohesion of regions in the EU. The priority 'regional competitiveness and employment' resembles Objectives 2 and 3 but with more stress being placed on the ideals articulated in the Lisbon strategy. Finally, space plays an enhanced role in the new report, with Urban, Equal, Leader+ and especially Interreg being elevated to the status of the Structural Funds Objective 'European territorial cooperation' (European Commission 2004a). Again, as in all preceding periods, the budget is being increased substantially, to about 384 billion Euros (European Commission (2004b).

Consequences for the Netherlands

It is hard to measure the exact spatial impact of EU regional policy in the Netherlands. Its effect is obviously less visible than in cohesion countries such as Greece and Spain, which have received more regional funds for physical infrastructure such as roads and railways (de Vet and Reincke 2002: 14). Much of the aid received by the Netherlands takes the form of support for training programmes or research and coordination under Interreg rather than physical infrastructure. Besides, in more affluent nations like the Netherlands, support via the Structural Funds is not only likely to be less extensive and manifest, but also raises the important issue of whether the developments would have occurred without EU support anyway (this is, of course, true to a certain extent for all Structural Funds recipients): the Structural Funds mainly assist the implementation of planned projects rather than generating completely new ones. This section examines the various ways the EU has invested in the development of the Netherlands in the framework of its regional policy, focusing on the previous and current Structural Funds periods.

Previous period: 1994-1999
According to an evaluation of the 1994-1999 Structural Funds period in the Netherlands, European funds were found to have contributed to a significant overall drop in unemployment in the targeted areas (ERAC 2003: v). This has been attributed to successful stimulation programmes co-financed by the EU, but we cannot confirm this because we do not know for certain what would have happened in these regions without EU support. A comparison with non-supported regions, performed by ERAC, revealed a mixed picture: in some sectors unsupported regions outperformed supported regions, in others they were similar, and in still other sectors, regions receiving EU aid outperformed non-supported regions. Regarding the last group, the EU funds that seem to have had the most positive effect were for transport, storage and communication projects. More importantly in a spatial sense, regions enjoying EU support allocated more land (in both absolute and relative terms) to the development of business parks (ERAC 2003: 29). One should, however, be cautious in drawing conclusions from the results of this kind of research because it is difficult to compare regions with different growth rates. Moreover, the question remains whether the Netherlands would have supported these areas anyway without EU aid.

The effects of EU policies are more readily discernable when they diverge from national policy. In this sense, the effect of EU regional policy is perhaps more evident in the Netherlands than other 'wealthy' Member States because it does not exactly match national spatial economic policy. In fact, the very concept of cohesion, far from being an exciting new policy frontier, seems somewhat of an anachronism in the Netherlands: it resembles national planning of three decades ago (Faludi and Zonneveld 1998a).

Nowhere is the disparity in policy objectives more visible than in the province of Flevoland, the only Objective 1 region in the Netherlands during the 1994-1999 period (and receiving phasing-out funds in the current period). The region was awarded Objective 1 status not because it was so backward, but because it simply met the requirements for having a low GDP per capita. Many Flevoland residents commute to other areas (mainly to Amsterdam) for work and, in the eyes of the EU, this means that economic production in the province is comparatively low. Consequently, the programmes submitted for EU focus on job creation within the province, partly through the construction of new business parks. Joke van den Brink, programme manager for European subsidies in Flevoland, estimated that EU assistance resulted in 25,000 extra jobs in the province. In addition, EU funding allowed the Eemnes A27/A6 motorway interchange (Almere Buiten) to be completed fifteen years ahead of schedule (Boiten and Van der Sluis 2000). Thus, if we attribute the growth in jobs in the Flevoland Objective 1 region in part to the efforts of the European Union, and factor in the additional capacity provided by the A27, one could argue that the main roads out of the region are less congested than they would have been without EU support.

Spatial effects in other regions in the 1994-1999 period include the co-financing of the N391 road in Drenthe, which redirects through traffic around the sensitive villages. Like Eemnes, this was primarily a matter of time: the project had been on the table since 1985, but was only started once it received EU funding in 1998. Other examples include support for a plant specialised in sieving powders in Limburg, a public transport shuttle service in the Noord-oostpolder, the 2100 ha nature reserve 'Gelderse Poort' in Gelderland and rural tourism in Drenthe (European Commission 2001b).

Current period (2000-2006)
Until about 1990, the Netherlands was a net recipient of European funds, but since then the Dutch position has gradually worsened (Ministerie van BZ 2002: 48). Whatever benefits the Netherlands may gain from the Structural Funds, agricultural policy and other support it receives, the fact remains that this in no way compensates for Dutch contributions. At present, the Netherlands is the largest net contributor to the EU.[1] In the next Structural Funds period (2007–2013) the Netherlands will receive no Objective 1 (i.e. convergence) funding at all and levels of Objective 2 and 3 (i.e. regional competitiveness and employment) funding may also fall as a result of positive employment development in relation to other EU countries (ERAC 2003: 39). This may help to explain the Dutch Government's current stance of targeting EU regional policy funds to the poorest Member States, rather than allowing them to circulate among the wealthier countries as well.

It is interesting to note that over half of all the Structural Funds received by the Netherlands in this period were for the Objective 3 programme. Since Objective 3 is not area-based, its spatial effects, along with some Community Initiatives like Equal, are difficult to trace. The maps in Figure 5 show the regions receiving area-based Structural Funds in the previous and current periods. These maps should still be read with caution: although the investment of funds into a particular area is bound to have spatial effects, it is extremely difficult to determine the exact extent of this effect, especially when the programmes have economic rather than spatial goals. Nonetheless, the difference in designation criteria are immediately apparent: the Objective 1/ phasing-out region of Flevoland corresponds to established administrative boundaries, while the other Objective designations show a more scattered

1. This is not merely a reflection of the relatively affluent position of the country, as the even more affluent Luxembourg is the largest net recipient of EU funds (Ministerie van BZ 2002: 47). However, in general, if the wealth of EU regions are empirically set against the levels of EU support they receive, a clear negative relationship is discernable (De Mooij and Tang 2002: 12).

Table 3. Structural Funds received by the Netherlands

Regional policy (2000-2006 period)	Budgeted amount (in euros)
Structural Funds	
– Objective 1 (Flevoland, phasing-out)	126 million
– Objective 2 (restructuring)	
North	342 million
East	142 million
South	140 million
Cities	200 million
– Objective 3 (employment and training)	
Single programming document ESF	1750 million
Community Initiatives	
– Interreg III	[824 million, shared]
– Urban II	9 million
Community Initiative Amsterdam	9 million
Community Initiative Rotterdam	12 million
Community Initiative Heerlen	
– Leader+ (rural development)	25 million
North programme	19 million
East programme	19 million
South programme	19 million
West programme	
– EQUAL (equal opportunities)	32 million
Equal programme	
– FIFG (fisheries)	32 million
Total Structural Funds [not including Interreg]	**2 876 million**

Source: Tweede Kamer (2002: 5-6)

pattern, with the Objective 2 and 5b areas from the previous period often (but not always) corresponding to Objective 2 areas in the current period.[2] A notable difference is the addition of cities such as Amsterdam in the current period.

Objective 1: Flevoland
As mentioned above, the province of Flevoland qualified for Objective 1 status in the 1994–1999 period, and thus for phasing-out funding in the current period. The total budget for the programme is 471 million Euros, of which 126 million Euros is contributed by the EU and about 15 per cent from the private sector (European Commission 2003a). The stated goals of the projects funded by EU regional policy include the development of rural and urban areas, strengthening the production sector, social cohesion and technical support. In the city of Almere alone, about twenty current projects have received EU funding (about 10% on average). Examples include a World Trade Centre, various walking routes, two railway stations and regeneration of the harbour with space provided for artists. The programme includes the construction of Kamer 2002: 9).

2. Unlike Objective 1 areas, Objective 2 status is awarded to defined areas, which are usually not consistent with administrative boundaries.

Figure 5. Areas receiving Structural Funds aid in previous and current periods

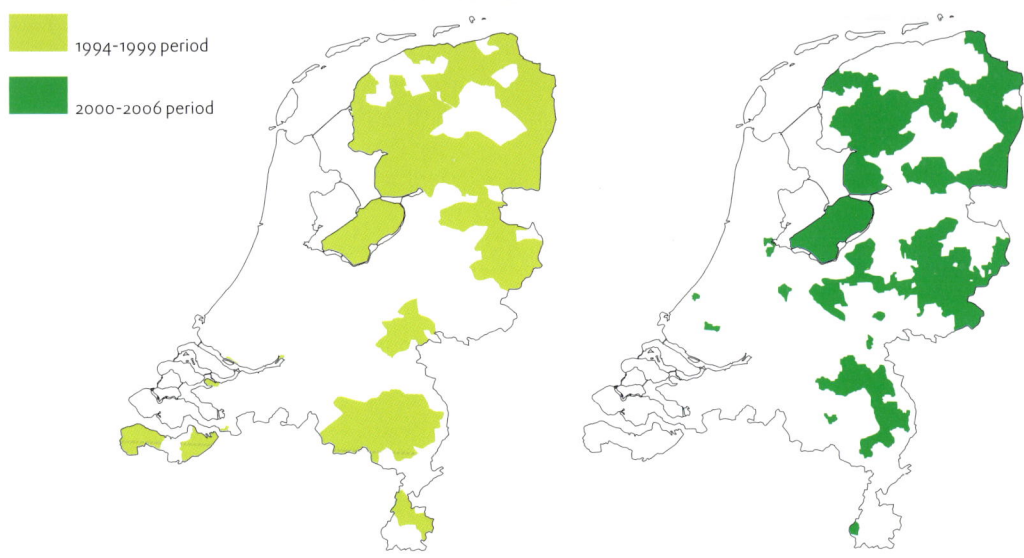

Source: ERAC (2003)

Objective 2: North Netherlands
The 'Kompas voor het Noorden' programme covers the three northern provinces of Drenthe, Friesland and Groningen. The primary goal is to bring the level of economic development (measured in jobs) in this region into step with the rest of the country. The EU funds for this programme are derived from various sources: Objective 2, phasing-out of Objective 2/5b programmes, Objective 3, funds from the EU agricultural policy, Leader+ and Interreg IIIA (SNN 2003: 11). Like many other Dutch programmes using Structural Funds, many of the effects are not directly reflected in changes in land use. Of the spatial effects, the most noteworthy are the development of business parks, the construction of infrastructure for recreational ends (cycle paths, nature trails and water routes) and the preservation of historic monuments. The programme makes provisions for the addition of 230 ha of new business parks in the current period (Tweede Kamer 2002: 9).

In 2003, the consultancy firm Ecorys conducted a midterm review of this programme. Although the criteria primarily relate to economic development, some spatial implications can be assumed as well. In view of the causality problem, Ecorys considered the developments that would not have occurred without the assistance of the 'Kompas' programme. Roughly speaking, these are 'the initiation of important developments which are not taken up when more urgent, but less important, matters are given priority within the regional budgetary parameters' (Ecorys 2003: 15). Specific projects include investments in knowledge and IT infrastructure, the Frisian 'Merenproject' for water recreation and the prestigious 'Blauwe Stad' residential development. In general, the 'Kompas' was found to be effective in stimulating economic development and all participating provinces have seen rapid growth in tourism.

There has been some criticism, though. By lowering development costs, EU subsidies may also remove the incentive for intensifying land use, resulting in lower densities in business parks. The workings of the real estate market itself can even be disrupted: although the intention is to attract businesses from outside the region, local businesses can simply relocate to the subsidised parks, leaving empty offices behind. Even when this is not allowed, artificial overproduction can threaten the viability of new parks. A case in point is the International Business Park Friesland. This park was developed with generous public funding (including EU Structural Funds) to attract multinational businesses to the region, but the only occupant (the computer assembler SCI) has since shifted its operations to Eastern Europe. Since the EU has decided not to demand repayment of its subsidies if the park is sold off in parcels to smaller businesses, the municipal council is now considering this option. A probable consequence is that the park would no longer be in a position to fulfil its original purpose of attracting international businesses.

Objective 2: East Netherlands
The programme for the eastern part of the Netherlands covers the provinces of Gelderland and Overijssel and part of the province of Utrecht. These provinces began lobbying for EU funds for the regeneration of problematic urban areas at the beginning of the previous Structural Funds period (1994). Although the emphasis lay in the economic sphere, the programme had a spatial component, which consisted mainly of the construction of new business parks and other development opportunities associated with the 'Betuwelijn', the dedicated freight-only railway line from Rotterdam to Germany.

In the current period, rural restructuring was successfully added to the programme; both here and in Zuid Nederland, intensive livestock farming must be reduced to meet EU nitrate standards (see the chapter on 'Water'). The construction of the multimodal transport terminals in Arnhem–Nijmegen and Twente, with EU financial aid, will have potentially large spatial effects by virtue of the physical construction itself and also by attracting related industrial activities (Boiten and van der Sluis 2000). In addition, a centre for sustainability in Zutphen is being supported with EU funds. EU funds are also being used to co-finance tourist activities, such as a pier for cruise ships on the Pannerdensch canal, walking routes on church paths and the renovation of a historic courtyard at Doornenburg Castle. In total, the region stands to receive 141 million Euros in EU funding towards its 391 million Euros budget for economic diversification.

Objective 2: South Netherlands
Limburg was early in lobbying the EU for development funds, receiving 40 million Euros in the first Structural Funds period and 100 million Euros in the second. Projects co-funded by the EU include 'Toverland' in Sevenum, the 'Mijn op Zeven' tourist centre in Ospel, a container terminal/industrial area in Holum, the 'Mondo Verde' theme park in Kerkrade and the 'Bassin' marina in

Maastricht. The area affected by the EU funding is significant: 3157 hectares of land will be developed for new uses or have existing uses upgraded in the current period (Tweede Kamer 2002: 9).

Objective 2: Cities
Nine Dutch cities now qualify for funding under Objective 2 Cities: Amsterdam, Rotterdam, The Hague, Utrecht, Enschede, Arnhem, Nijmegen, Eindhoven and Maastricht. Amsterdam receives approximately 34 million Euros for the Objective 2 areas Bijlmer/Amstel and Groot-oost and more through the Community Initiative Urban I and II (see below). Projects co-financed in the Zuidoost district by the EU include a recreation and sports facility, a children's circus, a business advice centre, a local employment centre and a women's empowerment centre. The Hague has used its Objective 2 funds to develop a complex for business start-ups and urban regeneration/public safety projects in the Haagse Markt and other areas. In all, the current Objective 2 programme for the cities envisions the renewal of 21 ha of urban public space in the current period (Tweede Kamer 2002: 9).

Community Initiative: Urban II
Urban seeks to improve conditions in Europe's most deprived urban areas. Implementation is decentralised, and carried out in partnership with other actors, such as the private sector and community groups (European Commission 2002a: 22). To qualify for funding, unemployment and crime levels must be twice that of the EU average and/or the areas must have a large immigrant population. The Netherlands receives 29 million Euros under Urban II for areas in three cities: Amsterdam, Rotterdam and Heerlen. The Amsterdam Urban II programme is the largest in Europe in terms of population. Interestingly, Heerlen received more money through this programme than Amsterdam or Rotterdam. Urban has a clear spatial impact, with physical and environmental regeneration making up 40 per cent of all spending. The first evaluation of Urban II was positive, but vague on the total added value of EU involvement, focusing instead on the added value of Urban in relation to other Structural Funds programmes.

Community initiative: Interreg III
The Interreg Initiative seeks to improve cohesion between Member States. It consists of three parts: Interreg III A funds are directed to cross-border areas, Interreg III B funds to transnational cooperation and Interreg III C funds to interregional cooperation.

Most Member States have seized the opportunity to initiate a number of Interreg III A programmes, including the Netherlands, which will draw an estimated total of 349 million Euros of the 4.875 billion Euros available (European Commission 2001a). Figures 6 and 7 give a few examples of how this money has affected spatial developments in the Netherlands.

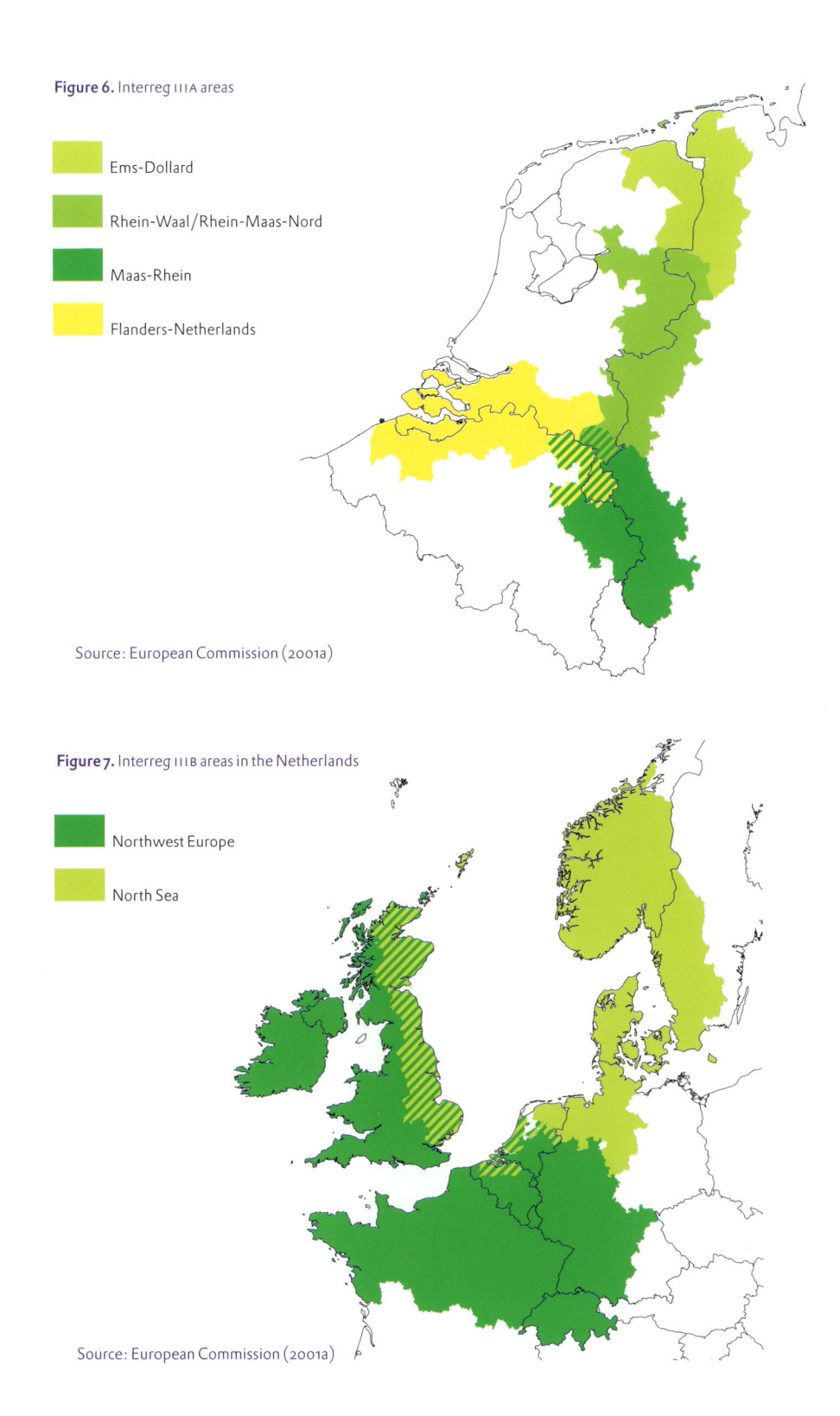

Figure 6. Interreg IIIA areas

- Ems-Dollard
- Rhein-Waal/Rhein-Maas-Nord
- Maas-Rhein
- Flanders-Netherlands

Source: European Commission (2001a)

Figure 7. Interreg IIIB areas in the Netherlands

- Northwest Europe
- North Sea

Source: European Commission (2001a)

38 · 39

Table 4. Description of Dutch Interreg IIIB programmes

Interreg IIIA

The Ems Dollart project (blue) focuses on infrastructure, cross-border economic and technological cooperation, environmental protection, human resources and integration.
 EU contribution: €35 million

The Rhine-Waal/Rhine-Meuse-Nord project (15 on map) focuses on economic development, employment, the environment, spatial planning, innovation, culture and tourism.
 EU contribution: €98 million

The Maas-Rhine project (green) concentrates on infrastructure, economic and scientific cooperation, environment (including agriculture), labour market and socioeconomic integration.
 EU contribution: €53 million

The Flanders-Netherlands border project (yellow) focuses on infrastructure, economic and technical cooperation, environment, training and labour market, and social integration.
 EU contribution: €84 million

Interreg IIIB and IIIC

The Interreg IIIB North Sea Region programme sponsors projects in the Netherlands ranging from water quality to short-sea shipping routes, urban water systems, and help with implementing the Water Framework Directive.
 EU contribution: €129 million

The Interreg IIIB North West Europe programme concentrates on cities and regions, accessibility, water management, sustainable development, heritage and trans-sea cooperation. The Dutch 'Green Heart' area has benefited from this in the framework of the 'Sustainable Open Space II' project. Other investments concern an ecological link along the Runde and new greenhouse developments near Emmen.
 EU contribution: €330 million

Interreg IIIC projects in which Dutch regions are taking part include CoPraNet (good practice in coastal management), MiluNet (multifunctional and intensive land use) and EcoNet (sustainable development and good practice in ports).
 EU contribution: €95 million

Source: Tweede Kamer (2002: 6); European Commission (2003a)

European Investment Bank

Whereas the Netherlands may not receive many subsidies compared with Greece or Spain, it has profited from long-term loans provided by the European Investment Bank (EIB), which issues credit to promote balanced development in the EU. These loans do not have to meet the criteria of regional policy and can be quite substantial. In the Netherlands, approximately 150 million Euros was borrowed from the EIB for the construction of the fifth runway at Schiphol airport, and Dutch banks borrowed another 262.5 million Euros from the EIB for small and medium-sized businesses. Another 80 Euros million was borrowed to modernise the Noord-Holland waste facility, 35 million Euros for the Zuid-Holland dune water company and 10 million Euros was borrowed for the Drenthe water supply company (European Commission 2003a).

Impact on planning practice

Besides the physical impacts, the process of gaining EU funding for regional development programmes can influence the way planning is done, and may thus affect future land use decisions. EU regional policy stimulates cooperation between all kinds of parties at the regional level, and in many countries constitutes the only form of regional strategic development.

Many have argued that EU regional policy has affected relationships within the public sector (e.g. Tewdwr-Jones and Williams 2001). In the municipalities of Heerenveen and Emmen, for example, the EU requirement for a public-private partnership led to the inclusion of the private sector in the development of holiday homes (Boiten and Van der Sluis 2000). To meet EU criteria to receive funding, the province of Gelderland had to make the concept of sustainable development more explicit in its plans than it had been before. This has brought about a shift in mentality, and future plans will probably also include the concept of sustainable development in the sense intended by the EU. Having participated in several Interreg projects, the province of Noord-Brabant has included cross-border thinking and action as one of the guiding principles in its regional plan (Heijmerink 2002: 142).

Experience with obtaining funds from Brussels has also lessened the habit of approaching national government for assistance. Larger cities and provinces are becoming more involved with the EU and many have assigned staff to investigate the best ways to obtain EU funds or work as lobbyists. Nevertheless, knowledge about the EU remains rather patchy in Dutch local government and is even a non-issue in smaller municipalities. The provinces seem to be more aware of EU issues and more willing to cooperate to achieve mutual goals. For example, the provinces of Overijssel and Gelderland have already joined forces as 'East Netherlands' when dealing with Brussels, and have recently raised their profile with the addition of Nordrhein-Westfalen as a partner. One provincial representative from Gelderland reports that it is imperative to coordinate efforts between organisations and governmental tiers in your own country when bidding for loans because 'on the chessboard of Europe if you don't form a united front, you'll be played off against each other.'

Although all this seems to point to a clear shift in intergovernmental relations in the Netherlands under the influence of EU regional policy, there are indications that this may only be a temporary arrangement. R.A.A. de Rooij pointed out in his PhD thesis that the Dutch national government (Ministry of Agriculture, Nature and Food Quality) recently reasserted its position by bundling projects and submitting them to the EU. In addition, national legislation on the supervision of European subsidies (*Wet toezicht Europese subsidies*) grants the national government the authority to make binding decisions about how EU funds are managed and spent, and can pass on any fines incurred to lower tiers (de Rooij 2003). Of course, the provinces oppose this, and their representative body in Brussels is resisting this 'nationalisation of regional policy'.

Conclusions

EU regional policy seeks to reduce regional disparities by funding economic development projects in underprivileged regions. Whether and how this occurs remains a subject of debate. There is widespread disagreement about the effectiveness of regional policy, both at the EU level and in the Netherlands, and some criticism can be directed at the criteria used to determine whether a region is underprivileged. According to the EU, which uses GDP per capita as an indicator, the wealthiest region in the Netherlands is Groningen and the poorest is Flevoland – which flies in the face of common knowledge.

Significant changes are imminent in European regional policy. The enlargement of the EU, the ongoing ESDP process, the Convention and the Lisbon strategy have all necessitated some kind of reform of regional policy. In the negotiations, the self-interest of some Member States is only thinly disguised by appeals to common discussions and concepts. The Dutch Government's position in this has been to end the money-go-round of providing aid to regions in wealthy Member States. Together with countries such as France, Britain and Germany, the Dutch Government is pressing for more assistance to regions with economic potential rather than to disadvantaged regions, pointing to the philosophy articulated in the Lisbon Protocol (of course, this viewpoint is not necessarily shared by lower tiers of government, or by some national ministries who stand to lose from a reduction in regional aid). For this reason, the reforms to the regional policy described in the *Third Report on Economic and Social Cohesion* have been criticised for not going far enough to end the European money-go-round (see Tweede Kamer 2003-2004, 21501-20, nr. 240).

Spatial impacts
Although quite extensive in terms of measuring job creation, the evaluations of Structural Funds in the Netherlands give little indication of how much the EU has affected spatial development. The main points of agreement seem to be the creation of new alliances in the public sector (how durable these are is unclear), new priorities as a result of conditions placed on funding, and perhaps the construction of more business parks, cycle paths and job training centres than would have occurred otherwise (Louwers 2003). Some argue that this has had a positive economic impact, while others claim that it merely represents a reshuffling of regional businesses accompanied by a general lowering of commercial land values, and hence building densities.

Further research
The impact of the Structural Funds in the Netherlands is a potentially interesting topic for future in-depth research. The age of Dutch Structural Funds may largely be over after 2006. At the same time, the current administration has discussed discontinuing support for weaker regions – particularly in the North – in favour of economically strong ones: the European philosophy of cohesion seems to have gained little ground in the Netherlands. This shift in policy generates some fruitful research topics: what is the effect of this for former recipients, and what does this say about the effectiveness of regional policy? By the same token, the impact of EU regional policy on planning processes in the Netherlands is also an interesting area to explore further. Although the new 'convergence' and 'competitiveness' Structural Funds priorities may yield less than in previous periods, and hence reduce the desire to invest in Brussels lobbies, the 'territorial cooperation' priority might be seized upon to forge new (international) alliances. This will certainly have an impact on administrative relationships, and indirectly on spatial development.

Transport

TRANSPORT

Introduction

At first glance, one would assume that, of all the policy fields examined in this survey, EU transport policy would have the most visible imprint on spatial developments in the Netherlands. After all, EU transport policy is well-developed and spatially relevant. Peters (2003) even considers the core idea behind the Trans-European Networks (TENs) to be the only functional EU spatial policy concept. Transport also seems to be a promising policy area to explore because transport infrastructure projects have a very clear-cut effect on land use: the insertion of roads, bridges, rail tracks and the like into the topography of a country not only creates new connections, but can also sever others by throwing up physical barriers. New transport links or the improvement of existing links affect the volume and flow of traffic and preferences for transport modes. High-speed train technology, for example, has 'shrunk' the European Union by reducing travel times between stations, as illustrated by time–space maps (e.g. Vickerman et al. 1999); this has potentially far-reaching implications for economic, social and cultural behaviour. In spatial terms, by changing the accessibility of a particular location, new transport infrastructure can improve land values and create new nodes of economic activity by making locations suitable for offices, shopping centres and other commercial facilities. At the same time, the spaces between nodes can suffer from a relative reduction in accessibility, putting them at a disadvantage. New infrastructure can also generate environmental impacts by increasing air and noise pollution, despoiling the landscape and reducing the liveability of the urban environment (Bruinsma et al. 2002).

Despite the obvious spatial implications of this area of European policy, it is not always clear how the objectives formulated at the EU level are translated into concrete spatial projects. It is also difficult to gauge the extent to which EU policy may have caused changes that would otherwise not have occurred. This chapter explores this issue further by discussing the degree to which EU transport policy has influenced spatial developments in the Netherlands.

EU policy

There are various reasons why transport is a policy topic at the European level. The European Union faces a dramatic rise in mobility and traffic: over the past thirty years the number of private cars on the roads has tripled and the action radius of most households has expanded considerably. Although this trend seems to have stabilised somewhat in the existing Member States, mobility in the accession countries is expected to grow rapidly. But increased demand has not affected all transport modes equally: from 1990 to 1998 road transport grew by 19.4 per cent, while rail transport actually dropped by 43.5 per cent (European Commission 2001c: 13-16). Recently published figures on expected increases in freight transport between 2010 and 2020 are not reassuring: road transport in the existing Member States is set to rise by as much as 65 per cent and by 135 per cent in the accession countries (High Level Group 2003). (Of course, this increase is partly a result of the EU's own internal market and transport policies, such as the harmonisation of technical and safety standards.) All this seems to indicate that a concerted effort is required to prevent unacceptable levels of congestion on Europe's roads. Considerable efforts will be needed to counterbalance the trend towards increased road use, by improving rail links and waterways, and to accommodate inevitable future growth in traffic.

Figure 8. Passenger Traffic Growth in the EU-15

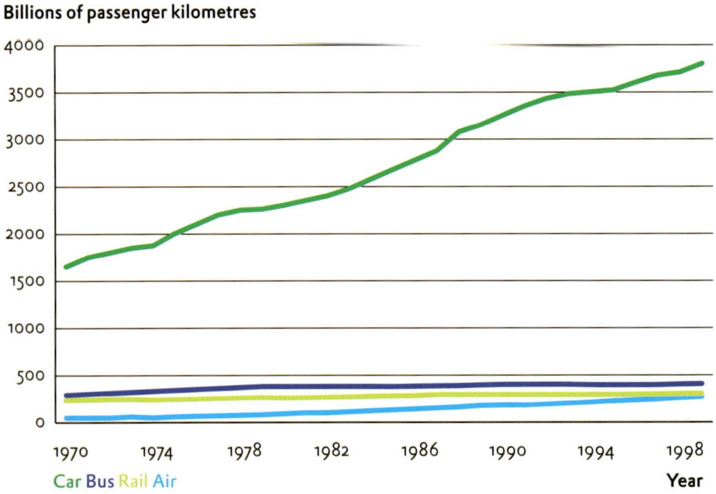

Billions of passenger kilometres

Car Bus Rail Air

Source: European Commission (2001c: 22)

Other reasons why the EU has become active in the area of transport are that an efficient transport system is a vital condition for future *economic growth*, and improved cross-border transport infrastructure will facilitate the movement of goods and passengers between Member States – a primary goal of the *common market*. In fact, EU transport policy has its roots in the desire to eliminating technical differences in transport legislation between Member States (Buunk 2003: 25). As we saw in the previous chapter, transport policy is often used as an instrument of *regional policy* as well, and considerable amounts of the Structural and Cohesion Funds are allocated to infrastructure projects to produce a level playing field. Some also argue that EU transport policy contributes to EU *environmental policy* goals as well, for example by shifting transport from road to rail. These various justifications for EU transport policy are made explicit in a statement of goals by the European Commission:

UNSEEN EUROPE

In contributing to the implementation and development of the internal market, as well as reinforcing economic and social cohesion, the construction of the trans-European transport network is a major element in economic competitiveness and a balanced and sustainable development of the European Union.[1]

But is this apparent synergy between policy sectors real? Many have pointed out that rather than complementing one another, these facets of transport policy actually conflict, and that many of the assumptions on which EU transport policy rest are not backed up by empirical evidence. Rather than solving the congestion problem, for example, new infrastructure can encourage greater mobility, delivering at most a brief respite. More car mobility brings with it increased CO_2 emissions, noise and air pollution, and the construction of physical infrastructure can threaten natural habitats and despoil the landscape, which is hardly the intent of EU environmental policy (Minderhoud 1997; Kusiak 1997; Bruinsma et al. 2002).[2] Moreover, rather than promoting cohesion, EU transport policy may actually intensify regional disparities by exposing vulnerable markets to competition and allowing local resources to drain away (Committee on Spatial Development 1999: 15; Vickerman et al. 1999; Hajer 2000; Peters 2003).[3] The most recent and most thorough study of this subject to date is ESPON project 2.1.1. An interim report tentatively concludes that transport infrastructure has a very slight positive effect on economic development:

> The first observation is that, if temporary local effects during the construction period are left aside, the overall effects of transport infrastructure investments are small compared with those of socio-economic and technical macro trends... If one considers that under normal economic circumstances the long-term growth of regional economies is in the range between two and five per cent per year, additional regional economic growth rates of less than one or two per cent over twenty years predicted by the two models are less than spectacular – even though it can be argued that one or two per cent of total GDP of the 29 ESPON countries is a huge sum compared to the costs of the infrastructure. (ESPON 2003: 159)

These issues, still largely unresolved at the EU level, will be discussed below in the section on the consequences for the Netherlands.

Origins
Although a common transport policy has been provided for since the very beginning of European integration in 1956, it only became a reality after the Maastricht Treaty. Before this, the UN Economic Commission for Europe and the OECD/European Conference of Ministers of Transport had discussed the desirability of a pan-European transport network, but the emphasis was on non-spatial regulatory issues, such as harmonisation and taxation of transport services. Article 154 of the Maastricht Treaty changed this with the introduction of Trans-European Networks (TENs) as a spatial concept. These networks cover the areas of telecommunications, energy and transport infrastructure;

1. Overview of the Trans-European Transport Networks 'TEN-T', available at http://europa.eu.int/comm/ten/transport/index_en.htm

2. For example, in 1995 the European environmental organisation BirdLife estimated that 13% of the most important bird habitats lie within 10 km of the planned TENs, while Greenpeace maintains that the TENs will cause CO_2 emissions to rise by 60% instead of 40% (Minderhoud 1997).

3. Although it has been argued that TENs enhance cohesion by making peripheral areas accessible, this lacks empirical backing. Similarly, although the majority of current TEN priority projects are rail (9 of the 14), funding for these is limited to 60%; the vastly larger Cohesion and EDRF funds directed at transport were earmarked for road infrastructure, tipping the balance to about 3:2 in favour of road.

the last, the Trans-European Transport Network (TEN-T), receives 80 per cent of the TEN budget (Committee on Spatial Development 1999: 14) and encompasses roads, railways, waterways, airports, seaports and traffic management systems.

The TEN policy is more significant than its modest budget suggests.[4] Although TEN funds are mainly used for feasibility studies rather than financing actual construction, the designation of networks and priorities via the TEN policy offers a framework for channelling vastly greater sums of money through the Cohesion and Structural Funds (Faludi and Zonneveld 1998b) and via the European Investment Bank and European Investment Fund (Robert et al. 2001: 52). In addition to providing a link to EU grants and loans, the TEN policy has a symbolic value: the inclusion of a particular project in the TEN network – or, better still, as a priority project – is a powerful endorsement that can assist proponents in their efforts to garner support in their own country.

Like regional cohesion, transport policy has grown in importance and budget. In the two decades before the EU Treaty in Maastricht, Community transport sector allocations averaged less than 1 billion ECU annually; this increased substantially after the publication of the TEN master plans.[5] A milestone in the history of the TENs was the identification in 1994 of 14 TEN-T 'Essen' priority projects, to be realised before 2010 (two passing through the Netherlands); these were adopted by the European Parliament in 1996.[6] The ESDP has since lent further credence to transport by declaring its second policy guideline (after polycentricity) to be 'securing parity of access to infrastructure and knowledge' (Committee on Spatial Development 1999).

Current situation: 2000-2006

In 2001, six new priority projects and two extensions (none of which pass through the Netherlands) were identified in the White Paper *European Transport Policy for 2010: time to decide*, bringing the total up to twenty. In contrast to earlier objectives involving the connection of peripheral regions, the goals articulated in the current policy document are solving bottlenecks, sustainable development and preparation for the enlargement (European Commission 2001c) – although none of the six new projects actually lie within the accession countries.

The transport budget has continued to grow: approximately 18 billion Euros is now being invested by the EU in the 2001–2006 period (with some funding from the TEN programme, but most via the Structural/Cohesion Funds) and Member States are borrowing an additional 6.6 billion Euros from the European Investment Bank (Raad voor Verkeer en Waterstaat 2003: 38). Nevertheless, the costs of the projects seem to have outstripped the capacity of the public sector. Whereas TEN projects were originally intended to be entirely funded by the EU and Member States, backlogs and missed timetables have made it necessary to obtain contributions from the private sector, usually in the form of PPP constructions. The EU is currently considering setting up a guarantee fund to back PPPs for designated TEN-T projects.

4. For example, in the 1997–2000 period the TEN budget was a mere €1.8 billion, as opposed to the estimated €400 billion required to realise all ongoing and projected projects (http://europa.eu.int/comm/ten/transport/financing/figures_en.htm). The current budget has been increased to €4.6 billion, but this is still rather small when spread over six years and divided between fifteen Member States.

5. In the 1994–1999 Structural Funds period, TEN-T projects received 3.5 billion ECU from EDRF Objective 1, 5 billion ECU from the Cohesion Fund and, from 1995 to 1998, 1.34 billion ECU via a special TEN budget line. An additional €14.2 billion was loaned from the European Investment Bank for TEN projects in the 1994–1997 period. The Commission estimates that the TEN budget for 2000–2006 will amount to €5 billion.

6. Decision No 1692/96/EC of the European Parliament and of the Council of 23 July 1996 on Community guidelines for the development of the trans-European transport network. The main criterion used for selection seems to have been traffic intensity rather than the connection of peripheral regions, implying that 'in general, the regions that already possess an elaborate infrastructure system were selected to receive more' (Robert et al. 2001: 137). Moreover, the selection occurred from the bottom up, meaning that most TEN projects, including those in the Netherlands, were actually 'long-standing pet industry projects that had been heavily promoted by the industrial lobby for some time' (Peters 2003: 15).

Expectations

The most important structuring parameters for the future of the TENs are the enlargement, the implications of 'territorial cohesion' and the Lisbon strategy (European Commission 2003b). In the Summer of 2003, a 'High Level Group' chaired by Karel van Miert convened to reflect on European transport policy and propose new TEN-T priority projects for the 2010–2020 period. The group reported a 'worrying increase in traffic congestion in urban areas, but also a new phenomenon of congestion on the major arteries of the trans-European network' caused by missing links and a lack of interoperability (High Level Group 2003: 13). This concern is compounded by new prognoses of increases in traffic in present and future Member States over the coming decades (see Table 5).

Table 5. Freight traffic growth in the EU-15/25

Freight transport mode	Current Member States' rate of increase (2010–2020)	New Member States' rate of increase (2010–2020)
Road	67%	135%
Rail	76%	63%
Inland waterways	56%	157%
Total increase	68%	95%

Source: High Level Group (2003: 22)

Except for part of the 'Iron Rhine' railway line that connects Antwerp to the German Ruhr area, none of the High Level Group's new TEN-T rail/road priority projects will pass through the Netherlands. There are, however, some interesting developments over water that will affect the Netherlands (Meuse river project, Rhine–Danube link, Motorways of the Sea). The main objective seems to be to improve links between present and new Member States (High Level Group 2003: 32–38). The costs of all these new links are nothing short of astronomical: an estimated 235 billion Euros for the priority projects themselves and 600 billion Euros for the whole network. On 21 November, the European Commission gave its final response to the High-Level Group's suggestion in a communication intended to integrate transport policy with the Lisbon strategy. In this, the Commission identified fifty-six 'quick start' TEN-T projects that by and large correspond to the High Level Group's recommendations. Again, the only project to cross Dutch soil is the Iron Rhine rail freight route from Antwerp to the East. The limited utility of this line for the Netherlands, coupled with a rejection of the Amsterdam–Groningen–Hamburg magnetic train initiative, has understandably caused some disappointment.

Although many of the proposed projects reflect the need for less environmentally damaging forms of infrastructure than road and air, simply building more railway lines will have a marginal effect on modal shift; what is needed, according to the research institute NEA, is a complete package, including road charging policies (NEA 2003: 131). At the moment, the introduction of road

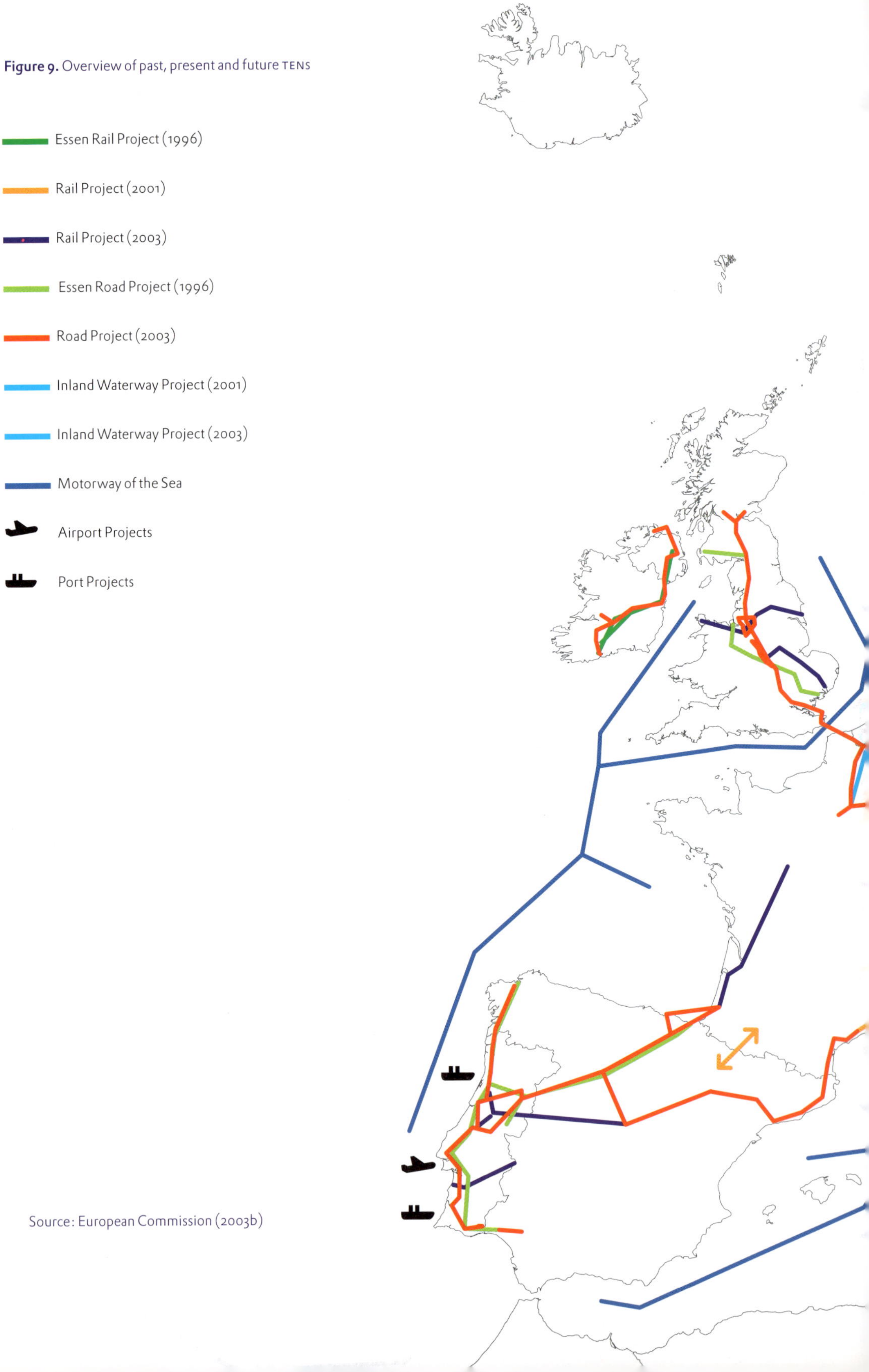

Figure 9. Overview of past, present and future TENS

- Essen Rail Project (1996)
- Rail Project (2001)
- Rail Project (2003)
- Essen Road Project (1996)
- Road Project (2003)
- Inland Waterway Project (2001)
- Inland Waterway Project (2003)
- Motorway of the Sea
- Airport Projects
- Port Projects

Source: European Commission (2003b)

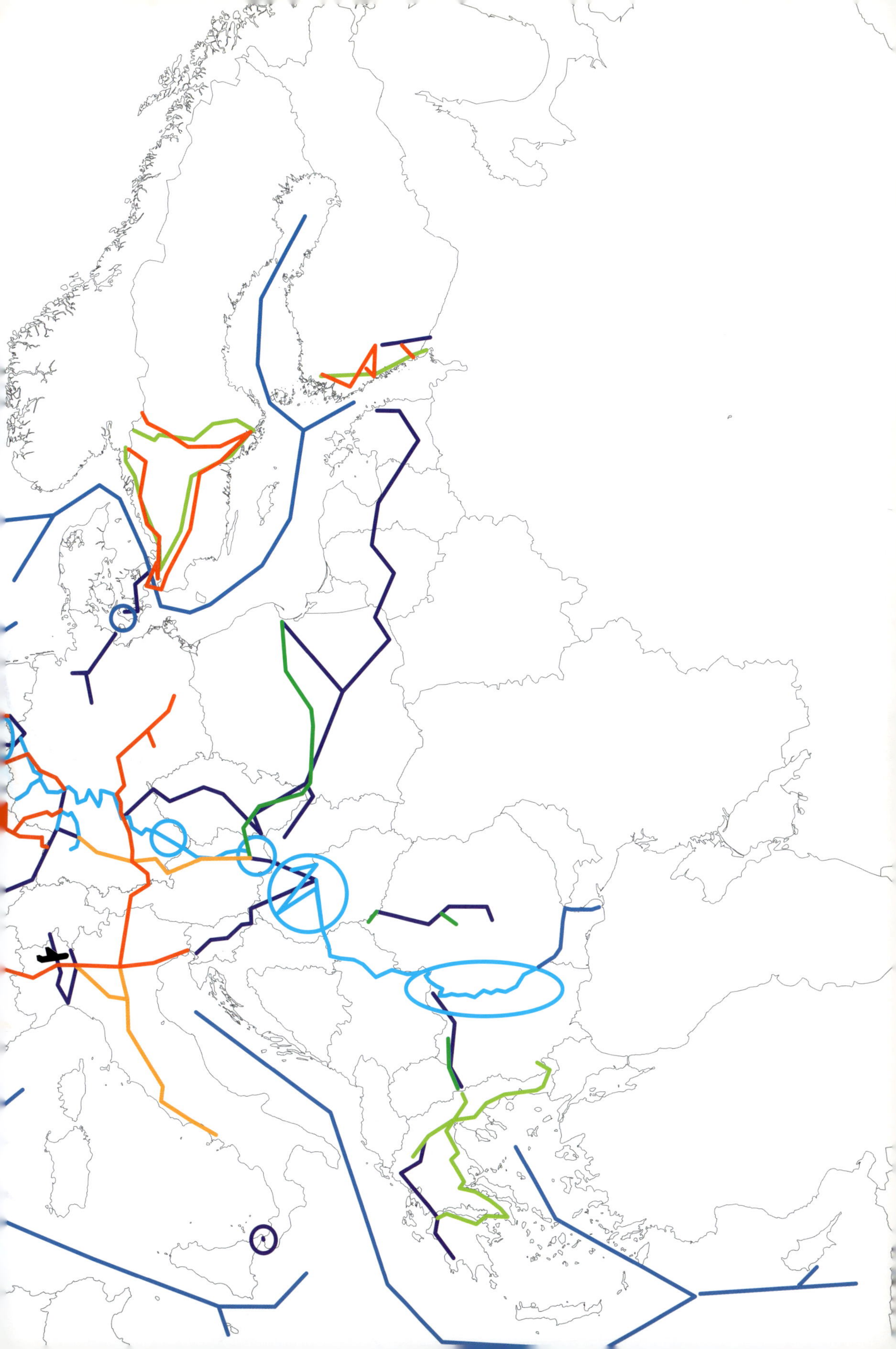

pricing is discretionary, to be decided by each of the Member States. The Netherlands has recently complained, for example, that the introduction of new tolls on German roads will encourage motorists near the border (especially in Limburg) to travel through the Netherlands. Although this lack of cross-border coordination could justify intervention at the EU level, road pricing remains a politically taboo subject in Brussels. The most definitive statement on this issue is the EC's intention of allowing Member States to use the extra charges collected from roads for the development of alternative transportation (the 'Eurovignette proposal', due in spring 2004).

As a final note, the EU seems to be taking steps towards abandoning its bottom-up approach to TEN-T designation in favour of a more strategic approach. At present, however, the share of EU contributions is simply too small to effectively sway a decision to carry out a particular project. The fragmented sources of EU financing (TEN-T, Structural Funds, EIB loans) can be better coordinated, and the EU proposes to raise the 10 per cent maximum contribution to 30 per cent for certain cross-border and broadband projects to expedite their implementation (European Commission 2003b). Although not mentioned in this document, the ESDP and any ESPON-informed update could also facilitate the development of a European strategic vision for a less bottom-up approach to identifying new projects.

Consequences for the Netherlands

Of the twenty TEN-T priority projects currently underway, only two are located in the Netherlands: the Paris–Brussels–Köln–Amsterdam–London high-speed passenger line (PBKAL) and the 'Betuwelijn' freight connection from Rotterdam to the German Ruhr area (see Figure 10). Although one could argue that both these projects are in line with Dutch national policy (and therefore, like all other TEN projects, not necessarily a product of EU policy), there was some direct funding from Brussels. In this section we concentrate on the physical impacts of these two developments and reflect on the possible impacts that other TENs (including those identified by the High Level Group) may have on the Netherlands.

South: high-speed passenger train (HST)
The PBKAL was launched in 1989 and so predates official TEN policy. Since its designation as a TEN, however, it has qualified for EU support. After many years of disagreement about its route, construction of the 102 km-long railway line began in 2000 and completion is planned for 2007, with a total investment in the Netherlands of approximately 4 billion Euros (European Commission 2002b: 12–13). In a treaty signed with Belgium (which came into force in 1999) the Netherlands has pledged to prepare, build, service and maintain the part of the line in its territory and ensure that the rest of the rail network is brought up to the standard required for the HST before 1 June 2005. The fact that the line will not be ready until at least 2007 has already led to some litigation (Klinge-van Rooij et al. 2003: 333–334).

Figure 10. Current TEN-T priority projects in the Netherlands

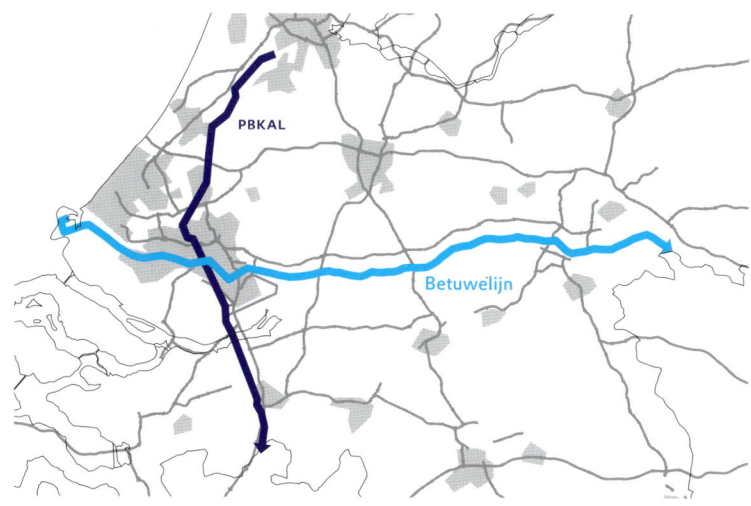

Source: European Commission (2002b)

In terms of direct spatial impact, one can argue that non-urban land along the 102 km-long route of the HST will be subjected to noise, risk and visual impacts – except, of course, where the line runs through the controversial eight-kilometre tunnel under the Dutch Green Heart. Indirectly, the line will change the time–space map of Europe, bringing Antwerp as close to Amsterdam South (one hour) as Den Bosch is today. The purpose of the line is to offer travellers an environmentally friendlier alternative to flying and driving, in part by linking a number of major European airports.

East: the Betuwelijn freight railway line
The other Dutch priority project is the 'Betuwelijn', a 160 km freight-only railway line from the port of Rotterdam to Germany, 112 km of which is new. It has also generated its share of controversy, more recently because of severe cost overruns.[7] The expected completion date is 2006. The project involves an estimated total investment of approximately 4.5 billion Euros, 80 million of which is being provided by the EU under the 2001–2006 TEN programme (European Commission 2002b: 18-19). The EU contribution is now less than 2 per cent of the total cost.

Although the direct spatial impact of the Betuwelijn resembles that of the HSL (adding approximately 100 km of new track in a country with the highest density of infrastructure in Europe), it has had a more difficult time overcoming political opposition. Part of this can be explained by the fact that, as a freight line, few people will personally experience any benefits. The project's value is sought primarily in the economic sphere. Specifically Rotterdam and Duisburg (Arnhem unsuccessfully lobbied for a Betuwelijn stop) are expected to profit from the Betuwelijn, and its logistical advantages could stretch as far as Eastern Europe and Italy. The importance of the Betuwelijn could increase further if the

[7.] Although the Betuwelijn has borne the brunt of the criticism, the PBKAL is perhaps even more severely over budget. An extra €985 million was reserved to safeguard both projects, two-thirds of which is for the Dutch part of PBKAL.

High Level Group's recommendation for a European freight rail network is
implemented (High Level Group 2003: 7).

Waterways
As we have seen, only two of the twenty TEN-T priority projects cross the
Netherlands. However, some interesting developments concerning water
transport will have spatial impacts in the Netherlands by increasing traffic
volumes on Dutch waterways and improving the economic position of some
Dutch logistics companies and the port of Rotterdam (see Chapter 'Spatial
policy issues and the EU'). For example, a recent EU directive aimed at
improving the position of the European inland shipping fleet has (inadvert-
ently) put Dutch logistics companies at an advantage (Raad voor Verkeer en
Waterstaat 2003: 34–35). Dutch shipping companies also stand to profit from
the Danube river improvement project, adopted in 2001, because it will allow
them to penetrate into Hungary and beyond. Incidentally, this is no small feat:
the proposed Main-Danube link has been an ambition since Charlemagne first
attempted it in 793 (Williams 1996: 92). The same is true for the newly
designated priority projects, such as the 'Motorways of the Sea' that links the
North Sea with the Baltic and South Europe, and the projects to resolve the
Rhine-Main-Danube bottleneck and develop short-sea shipping. At the same
time, the designation of rail and water TENs poses a threat to companies that
have carved out a prime position for themselves in road transport (Kusiak 1997:
15). We will return to these topics in Chapter 'Spatial policy issues and the EU'
when discussing the significance of EU policy for mainports.

Airports
Although not explicitly part of the TEN-T network, regional airports have
expanded with the growth of budget airlines, bringing about some important
shifts in passenger and freight traffic in Europe. Some of these connections
may even undermine the viability of some Community-supported TENs. This
point will be discussed further in the Chapters 'Competition policy' (competition) and 'Spatial policy issues and the EU' (mainports).

Conclusions

It is evident that the EU applies the subsidiarity principle more rigorously to the
TENs than to other policy sectors – intervening in matters only when absolutely
necessarily (Robert et al. 2001: 51). New priority projects are generally
designated from the bottom up, with national projects or initiatives being given
TEN status, rather than being determined at the EU level. Much of this has to do
with the level of EU funding in relation to the total cost. In this respect, recent
developments seem to indicate an increased willingness to raise the level of
funding (to 30%) in certain areas like border regions. These are usually
commercially unfeasible because national networks are poorly linked to their
neighbours (Robert et al. 2001: 43).

The immediate spatial impacts of new infrastructure are highly visible: new
links between remote areas, and sometimes local barriers. The more indirect or

unseen effects, on regional development and the environment for example, are more controversial. Nevertheless, new transport infrastructure financed by the Structural Funds continues to comprise an important part of regional assistance.

Spatial impacts
In terms of direct spatial impact in the Netherlands, European transport policy has so far not produced any significant changes in land use or planning processes. Transport remains primarily a national activity and both of the Essen priority projects that cross Dutch territory were existing national initiatives that later qualified for EU support (this, of course, is true for all TEN projects in the EU). Since less than 5 per cent of the total costs are covered by the EU, it has brought about no palpable changes in priorities or made much difference to the total viability of the projects.[8] The EU can have a greater impact on more uncertain projects, such as the proposed 'Zuiderzee magnetic train' link between Groningen and Schiphol. The recent decision not to designate this as a TEN-T priority project not only means the loss of a substantial sum of money (albeit still a small fraction of the total cost), it also casts doubt on the overall value of the connection. It could be argued, therefore, that projects with an official TEN label and financial support are more difficult to abort once they have been approved.

The indirect spatial impacts of EU transport policy might be more significant for the Netherlands. By improving international connections, TENs can influence the choice of transport mode made by people and businesses, and even the locational preferences of distribution companies. The Betuwelijn and improved waterways will affect the position of the port of Rotterdam, and the PBKAL the position of Schiphol Airport and cities near it. Because neither of these projects have been completed, it remains to be seen what the actual spatial effects will be, and whether they will raise the level of enthusiasm for TENs among Dutch policymakers. The TEN policy may be more important for the Netherlands as these networks are expanded eastwards. Decisions to promote road or rail, or the degree to which short-sea shipping or the Motorways of the Sea are successful, will influence strategic decision-making by Dutch logistics companies; viewed from the perspective of the Dutch transport sector, the TEN-T policy may offer an avenue for solving bottlenecks outside the Netherlands. Finally, TENs can also have a more conceptual impact. For some time 'corridors' were considered as a possible leitmotiv for spatial planning, reflecting the view that economic activities are more efficient when bundled along broad transport axes. Although this idea was abandoned as an official spatial concept by Dutch planners in the late 1990s, proponents of this idea can draw succour from EU policy, which draws a direct link between transport and economic development (van Duinen, forthcoming).

Further research
The discussion above has raised some interesting subjects for more in-depth research. For example, it would be interesting to investigate further what role the EU had, if any, in the PBKAL and Betuwelijn process. Another, more

8. On the other hand, by supporting the realisation of two railway lines, EU transport policy may have contributed in some small way to the further intensification of infrastructure density in a country where already 7.2% of the all land use is directly affected and 1.6% indirectly affected by the presence of physical infrastructure (Bruinsma et al. 2002). Land use along the two Dutch TEN routes will certainly be severely affected, but this is primarily a result of national rather than EU policy.

interesting, study would be to examine the impacts of decisions on TENs outside the Netherlands on Dutch companies (this subject will be returned to in the Chapters 'Competition policy' and 'Spatial policy issues and the EU').

Before embarking on such an endeavour, one must bear in mind that a great deal of information already exists on this subject and new studies on the impact of the TENs policy are being produced with great frequency, many by research institutes at the member state level[9], but also by ESPON.[10]

9. For example, TNO-Inro recently completed its IASON investigation of the impact of transport policies on short-term and long-term spatial development in the EU (commissioned as part of the Fifth Framework European Research Programme), and the research institute REA Transport and Research and Training BV will complete its scenario study of TENs in Europe, including the Netherlands, sometime in 2004.
10. Specifically its project 2.1.1 *Territorial Impact of EU Transport and TEN Policies*. The third interim report (used for this study) was published in August 2003, and the final version is expected sometime this year.

Agriculture

AGRICULTURE

Introduction

Although not necessarily the intention, European agriculture policy has arguably left a greater mark on the EU territory than any of the other sectoral policies investigated in this study. By setting prices on certain agricultural goods within the EU and raising trade barriers for outside producers, vast tracts of land could be cultivated profitably that would have otherwise been converted to some other use. Similarly, the abolition of tariffs within the confines of the EU has allowed farmers with superior techniques or more favourable conditions to outperform their competitors and expand their enterprises dramatically, usually resulting in growing economies of scale (i.e. larger but fewer farms), and geographical specialisation.

Since the 1990s the EU has been in the process of reforming its agricultural policy. This policy has been blamed for causing overproduction, environmental damage, running up the EU budget and more recently, distortion of the global marketplace. Price guarantees and tariffs are slowly giving way to direct aid to farmers and an increased awareness for sustainable development – and this change will surely have spatial consequences as well. The changes in agricultural policy will have significant spatial impacts because 43 per cent of the EU territory will be affected and because over half of all agricultural production in the EU (59% in production value) falls under the price guarantee mechanism. With the enlargement in May 2004, the percentage of the EU territory in agricultural use will increase. And because agriculture accounts for about 20 per cent of all employment in Poland, the Baltic states and Slovakia (in the Netherlands this is 3%) (Asbeek Brusse et al. 2002), it is no surprise that the negotiations held in recent years on the accession of the new Member States were largely about European agricultural policy. In mid 2003, following a mid-term review by the European Commission, new steps were taken towards further reform of the European agricultural policy, necessitated in part by the enlargement. This chapter examines the shifts in land use in the Netherlands which have occurred as an indirect result of past, recent and anticipated changes in European agricultural policy.

EU policy

The common agricultural policy (CAP) has its foundations in the Treaty of Rome (1957) establishing the European Economic Community (EEC). With the food shortages during and after the Second World War still fresh in the collective memory, self-sufficiency was a prime objective of the fledgling Community. The main goals of the common agricultural policy were to promote an efficient agricultural sector, provide a reasonable income for farmers and guarantee food supply for the European population at reasonable prices. The common market, with its protected external borders, was established to raise the level of production, the most important mechanism for achieving this being price support (in addition to import restrictions, export subsidies and income support). This, incidentally, was a costly endeavour: in 1970, the CAP took up 88 per cent of the total EEC budget. In 2002 agricultural expenditure still accounted for about 45 per cent of the EU budget, or 46 billion Euros (Ministerie van BZ 2003).

The CAP was so successful that within 20 years Europe was able to produce more than enough food for its own population, but at artificially high prices. Indeed, within 20 years, agricultural production in the Member States had grown so much that exports were rising sharply and surpluses mounting (e.g. the proverbial 'butter mountain' and 'milk lake'). The Netherlands Scientific Council for Government Policy (1992) and Professor A.M. van der Woude (1992) observed that, in time, the continuing rise in productivity could lead to about 30 to 40 per cent of European agricultural land being taken out of production because it would, in strict agricultural terms, become surplus to requirements.

It also became increasingly clear that the growth in production was being achieved at the expense of the landscape, nature and the environment. The EU reacted in stages to all these objections to its agricultural policy, first by raising prices and later by introducing production quota (milk quota were introduced in 1984) and linking income subsidies to measures designed to limit production, such as set-aside (i.e. paying farmers for not cultivating some of their land). Nevertheless, by the early 1990s the system of protected European markets was in danger of collapsing under the weight of its own success and was becoming too expensive to maintain. The pressure for reform was intensified further by the WTO/GATT (Uruguay Round) as the negative consequences for developing countries of the protectionist EU policy became clearer, an example being the 300 per cent import tariff on sugar (Asbeek Brusse et al. 2002). In response to these trends, the European Commission began a drastic shift in expenditure from production support to income support and rural development (the 1992 MacSharry reform).

Current and future policy
The current agricultural policy has continued in this vein, stepping up efforts to mitigate the various negative side effects of the CAP, such as overproduction, environmental damage and market distortion. The MacSharry reform of 1992 was a milestone in this process. Another was Agenda 2000, which put other agricultural policy themes in the spotlight:
– expanding (external) market orientation and competitiveness
– food safety and food quality
– stabilising farm incomes
– rural development and quality of life in rural communities.

The European Commission also agreed to simplify and further decentralise agricultural policy. Agenda 2000 also included a decision to hold a mid-term review (European Commission 2003f), which set out a number of steps towards further reform of the European agricultural policy, leading to the political accord by the Council of Agriculture and Fisheries Ministers (27 June 2003). This defined some important changes in the direction of agricultural policy, which were also needed to accommodate the expansion of the EU with the ten new Member States. The following are some of the key elements of the reform, which are due to come into effect on 1 January 2005:

– Decoupling of direct income support to farmers for production: in future, farm payments will not be linked to the amount of subsidised crops grown or the amount of livestock held; instead, the level of income support will be based on the amount of farm receipts in the past.
– Farm payments will be conditional on meeting 18 European directives and regulations in the field of the environment, natural habitats, animal welfare and animal health (cross-compliance).
– Member States may use up to 10 per cent of the farm payments as a national or regional 'envelope' to support specific forms of agriculture that benefit the environment, promote the quality of produce or market certain (e.g. regional) agricultural products.
– The direct payments to large agricultural enterprises will eventually be reduced (modulation) to allow money to be transferred to the 'second pillar' of EU agricultural policy: rural development policy. This will start at 3 per cent in 2005, rising by 1 per cent annual increments to 5 per cent in 2007. Each Member State will retain at least 80 per cent of these modulated agricultural funds.
– An extra stimulus for rural development policy, including the improvement of production and food quality, meeting EU standards on upkeep of the environment, animal welfare, and habitat and landscape management.

The heads of state had already decided at their meeting in Brussels in the autumn of 2002 that the EU agriculture budget would be frozen. The budget ceiling for the EU agricultural policy (excluding payments for the second pillar) was fixed at about 43 billion Euros per year until 2013, which means that all agricultural payments, including those for the new Member States, will have to remain under this level. In addition, numerous adjustments have been made to specific crop and sector premiums, the most important for the Netherlands being the drastic price reductions in the dairy sector (Bont 2003). Because this agreement still has to be worked out in more detail and allows the Member States a certain amount of flexibility in applying it in their own countries, the Ministry of Agriculture, Nature and Food Quality will produce its own policy vision on the concrete implementation of European agricultural policy in the Netherlands.

Consequences for the Netherlands

For foreigners it is hard to believe that the Netherlands, one of the smaller Member States in terms of land area, is the second largest net exporter of agricultural produce in the world (about €45 billion in 2001). Only the United States exports more. The most important export products are ornamental plants, meat, vegetables and dairy products. About 90 per cent of Dutch greenhouse horticultural produce (tomatoes, flowers, etc.) is exported. In the post-war era, Dutch agriculture experienced a period of rapid growth and intensification, encouraged by the open borders and agricultural policies of the EU. From 1950 to 1990 gross production volume grew by almost 3.5 per cent per year, while the area under agricultural production shrunk by 20 per cent; the number of people employed in agriculture fell by as much as 65 per cent, while the total number of agricultural enterprises fell from about 300,000 in 1960 to 97,000 in 2000 (Hamsvoort et al. 2002). An interesting body of literature has accumulated on the drastic consequences for the Dutch countryside of EU production support and the spectacular growth in productivity of the agriculture sector (e.g. *De graanrepubliek* by F. Westerman and *Hoe God verdween uit Jorwerd* by Geert Mak).

We have seen how, from the 1960s, the CAP has actively protected European agriculture with a system of price support, import restrictions and export subsidies. The most significant European support measures for the Netherlands were for grain production and dairy farming. In the 1970s and 1980s, when CAP expenditure was strongly tied to agricultural production (e.g. via the guarantee funds), EU agricultural policy was by far the most important source of EU funding for the Netherlands. Even in 2000, the Netherlands received more than 1.4 billion Euros from the EU agricultural budget, accounting for over half of all its receipts from the EU (€2.2 billion).

But that is not the whole story. Dutch agriculture is very different from that in other EU countries because only a quarter of the production value of Dutch agriculture falls under the EU's price guarantee mechanism (this is 59 per cent for the whole EU). For this reason, the opening of borders within Europe had an even more profound effect on Dutch agriculture. Even before the Second World War, the Netherlands was a net exporter of agricultural produce because of its favourable physical conditions, its location in the most densely populated part of Europe, the port of Rotterdam, and of course the high level of expertise in agricultural production. And the availability of cheap natural gas since the 1970s further stimulated the development of greenhouse horticulture. All these factors enabled the Dutch agricultural sector to react quickly to new export opportunities arising from European cooperation, allowing the Netherlands to reap the rewards of the open market and European agricultural policies (Bieleman 1992; Netherlands Scientific Council for Government Policy 1992). The expansion of export opportunities within the EU as a result of harmonisation laid the foundation for an explosive growth in agricultural production in the Netherlands. Since the 1990s, the gross added value of agriculture and horticulture has amounted to about 9 billion Euros annually (CBS 2003: 284), with greenhouse horticulture contributing the largest and most rapidly growing share, while livestock and arable farming are declining (Milieu- en Natuurplanbureau 2001). In addition, the common market was a major, indirect, stimulus for the growth in pig farming. Thanks in part to EU agricultural policy, the intensity of Dutch agriculture is now three times the European average, and still rising.

Spatial impacts
The close ties between European and national agricultural policies make it difficult to single out the spatial consequences of European policies in the Netherlands. Besides, economic concerns receive most attention. For example, greenhouse horticulture and intensive livestock farming (which incidentally do not fall under the price guarantee mechanism) are the most important sectors from an economic point of view, but take up relatively little space.

One way we can gauge the effect of the CAP in the Netherlands is to consider the kinds of produce that have received EU support. The following Dutch agricultural products fall under the price guarantee mechanism: starch potatoes, sugar beet, cereals and feed crops, dairy products, calves and cattle (SER 2003). For this study it was not possible to investigate how much of this increase in production was directly stimulated by EU agricultural policies; this is likely to be the case in the arable, dairy and intensive livestock sectors (Hamsvoort et al. 2002), but for horticultural products it is reasonable to assume that the open EU market and national policies (research, extension and education, rural land development and energy policies) are more important factors because there has been virtually no EU support for these crops. On the other hand, the increase in the area of fallow land seems to be a direct consequence of the EU payments for taking land out of production (set-aside) because there is no real agricultural need to do this in the Netherlands. The land area under agricultural use in the Netherlands is gradually shrinking, particularly the area of grassland and arable crops, while the area under field and greenhouse horticulture and set-aside is rising (see Figure 11).

Table 6. Agricultural land use since 1950

	Land area (1000 ha)						
	Arable	Grass	Horticultural crops				Total area
			Total	Field	Glass	Set-aside	
1950	930	1317	90	87	3	–	2337
1960	892	1327	98	93	5	–	2317
1970	694	1334	114	107	7	8	2143
1980	705	1198	113	104	9	5	2020
1990	799	1096	104	94	10	6	2006
2000	802	1018	119	109	11	23	1967

Source: Gordijn et al. (2003b)

In 2002 the Ministry of Agriculture, Nature and Food Quality drew up estimates of the spatial consequences for the Netherlands of EU agricultural policies (Massink and Meester 2002). These were based on calculations by the EU, the Agricultural Economics Research Institute (LEI) and the ministry's 'Expertisecentrum'. Although the data used do not entirely agree with the final national implementation of the June 2003 decisions on the reform of the EU agricultural policy, they do give a plausible picture of the possible long-term effects of the trend towards liberalisation, which is set to continue under pressure from the WTO. The general conclusion is that, even under full liberalisation, Dutch agriculture can maintain its competitive position in the world market, particularly in the dairy farming sector (assuming large farms with 200 to 1000 cows) and in the field and greenhouse horticulture sector. The Netherlands will eventually have two million hectares of fertile, easy-to-work and easily accessible agricultural land, centrally located within the most heavily urbanised part of the European market of more than 300 million consumers. Full liberalisation is expected to have favourable consequences for arable farming, beef production and the intensive livestock sector. This last sector, though, will not only have to deal with the changing market but will also face stricter animal welfare and environmental standards (see also Chapter 'Transport').

In an exploratory study of the future of Dutch agriculture, Hamsvoort et al. (2002) calculate that if the current trend of increasing the scale of production continues, only one third of the present number of agricultural and horticultural enterprises (97,000) will survive. A reduction in the number of dairy farms from 25,660 in 2001 to about 12,000–16,000 in 2010 is considered plausible, but does not necessarily have to lead to a comparable reduction in the amount of grassland because many dairy farmers are expected to turn to other livestock. Some will adopt diversified or 'multifunctional' farming systems that combine farming with recreational services, habitat and landscape management, regional products and even social care services, which offer farmers the opportunity to supplement their incomes to remain financially viable. The authors also calculate that in 2010, supported by the EU rural development policy, diversified agriculture will have expanded to about 55,000 ha, broken down into about 20,000 ha of new landscape elements, 10,000 ha under private sector habitat management and 25,000 ha of forestry crops on agricultural land. They estimate that some sort of diversification or multifunctional agriculture can already be found on more than a quarter of all farms in the Netherlands (van der Ploeg et al. 2002; see also Chapter 'Spatial policy issues and the EU'). A special consideration in the agricultural sector is the ageing of the farming population: 28 per cent of Dutch farmers are older than 55 and claim not to have a successor. For this reason alone we can expect structural changes in the sector; in the West and on the sandy soils in the East a significant proportion of diary farmers (33% and 11%) are prepared in principle to move towards some form of diversified farming (van Eck et al. 2002). Furthermore, land-based livestock and arable farming in the most densely populated areas of the country is under severe pressure from urban expansion and high land prices. At the same time, traditional agriculture in these areas is under extra pressure because the physical and spatial opportunities for expansion to raise output are not available.

Other studies suggest even more dramatic long-term effects on Dutch farming as a consequence of changing EU agricultural policies (Vereijken 2002; Kol 2001). In fact, in an article called 'Farming will disappear from the Netherlands', Vereijken and Agricola predict that in about ten years' time most farmers will have left the countryside. As indicators for this forecast they use the economic size of farm holdings, the economic intensity of agricultural land use per hectare and population density (or urban pressure) per hectare.

Based on two recent studies by the agriculture ministry's expertise centre, *Boeren op pad naar vrijhandel* [Farmers adapting to free trade] and *Vrijhandel, milieu, natuur en landschap* [Free trade, environment, nature and landscape] (Expertisecentrum LNV 2003a, 2003b), we can map out the following picture of the long-term future for each sector:

– Arable farming: a partial replacement of current grain crops with feed crops (grass, maize) and a slight decrease in areas producing sugar beets.
– Potatoes: the cultivation of starch potatoes (49,000 ha) will in time disappear from the Netherlands, while the area under seed and ware potatoes will remain more or less stable.
– Horticulture: the cultivation of field vegetables will come under pressure, but will be able to survive through further specialisation and an increase in the scale of production; the cultivation of other crops (bulbs, ornamental plants) and greenhouse crops is expected to increase in scale, but not much in area.
– Dairy farming: 75 per cent of milk production will become concentrated in very large farm enterprises (intensive units with cows in sheds); the remaining dairy farmers will continue with land-based production, breeding their own followers and putting cows out to pasture (approx. 2 per ha).
– Beef production: this will only be viable in combination with habitat management.
– Intensive livestock farming (pigs, chickens): the number of farms will be halved and production will fall to 75 per cent of current levels by 2010.

Based on the current distribution of agricultural activities we can indicate the spatial consequences of the trends outlined in this study for each region of the Netherlands (Table 7).

Table 7. Change in agricultural land use per region

Region	Change
North Netherlands	Increase in scale of arable production and very large-scale dairy farming
Flevoland	Arable and large-scale dairy farming
East Netherlands and South Limburg	Arable and dairy farming under considerable pressure, unless diversified farming is given the opportunity to develop
Sandy soils of Central Netherlands, North Limburg and Noord-Brabant	Arable farming under considerable pressure, concentration of intensive livestock farming, possibly also large-scale dairy farming
Clay soils of Noord-Brabant, West Netherlands	Large-scale arable farming and horticulture
Peat grasslands of West Netherlands	Rapid decline of dairy farming, unless this can be continued in an extensive form (own production of roughage, breeding followers), good opportunities for diversified farming

The scenario study *Ruimte voor Landbouw* [Space for Agriculture] by Alterra (van Eck et al. 2002) sketches four possible development trends for agriculture in the Netherlands, illustrated on maps (see Figures 11-14). These are based largely on the same data as the studies by the Ministry of Agriculture, Nature and Food Quality described above. In addition to economic factors, including the expected further liberalisation of the EU agricultural policy, Alterra also considered the possible influences of national and regional spatial, nature, environmental and water management policies. The study presents a strong regional differentiation of agricultural policy as an answer to the perceived need for a drastic reconsideration of the position of agriculture in the Netherlands, itself largely a consequence of the recent reform of European agricultural policy. It describes four conceivable development trends, for which the most favourable spatial configurations are shown on the illustrations of the different regions.

The agroproduction parks envisage a much tighter clustering of intensive livestock farms than the current plans for restructuring the agricultural areas in the provinces of Gelderland and Noord-Brabant and in North Limburg. This study explores the 'industrialisation' of this sector, in which the main elements in the production chain (animal feed, livestock farms, slaughterhouses and meat and manure processing) are located on industrial parks to optimise the use of energy and transport infrastructure and deliver the best possible benefits for the environment.

The growth of EU funds for rural development policy (the 'second pillar') could provide an extra stimulus for the last two categories (amenity agriculture and agri-environmental farming/landscape stewardship). The EU's three objectives for rural areas are:
1. strengthening the agricultural and forestry and sectors
2. making rural areas more competitive
3. conserving the natural and cultural heritage.

A recent study by the Agricultural Economics Research Institute (LEI) has revealed that the Rural Development Plan for the Netherlands 2000–2006, which sets out how this policy is to be implemented, allocates 73 per cent of the budget to the third priority. This also appears to be the most important objective in the regions examined in other Member States, with the exception of the more urbanised regions, such as Flanders, where strengthening the agricultural and forestry sectors has the highest priority (Terluin and Venema 2003).

A comparison of the results of these studies reveals three main spatial consequences for the Netherlands in the long term:
1. Land-based agriculture (dairy and arable farming): the increasing scale of production, high land prices and water management problems will gradually drive this form of agriculture out of the West and other urbanised areas. There are good opportunities for the dairy sector in North Netherlands; excellent opportunities for large-scale arable farming and field horticulture

will be found in Flevoland, the northern part of the province of Noord-Holland, Zeeland and the western part of Noord-Brabant.
2. Intensive livestock farming and greenhouse horticulture: increasing concentration in regional complexes (see Figure 12).
3. Diversified or multifunctional agriculture: good opportunities near urban areas and nature areas, and in coastal areas, the main river floodplains and (protected) landscapes.

These forecasts are based on continued liberalisation and a declining influence of EU agricultural policy. The changes in Dutch agriculture will be considerable, partly through intensification and diversified farming and partly through further intensification and specialisation. The agriculture ministry talks about dairy farmers with about 200 to 1000 cows (Massink and Meester 2002). This picture of the future also makes it clear how important diversified and multifunctional forms of agriculture will be from the landscape and spatial point of view. Urban residents that want access to open park-like landscapes around the cities may well be disappointed to find an increase in rather 'untidy' uses on vacant farm holdings (riding stables, caravan storage, haulage and builder's yards). Meanwhile, greenhouse horticulture remains firmly embedded in the most densely populated areas in the West and it is proving difficult to relocate these enterprises to areas with less development pressure (where land prices are lower).

So should we leave the decision on which type of farming develops where to farmers' initiatives and market forces, or should we exercise greater planning control over land use in rural areas? The evolving new water management policy will be a good means of steering land use in rural areas: more space will be needed in future for retaining and storing water and agricultural use will have to adapt to the requirements for improving water quality (see Chapter 'Water'). Regional spatial planning and local planning can be used to encourage favourable combinations of land uses, for example extensive farming with recreation, habitat management and certain forms of rural living; more focused use of EU funds for rural development could support this process. Spatial and economic considerations may require national guidance on the formation of the clusters of intensive farming units mentioned above (for which logistical aspects will be an important consideration) if the restructuring plans for the 'concentration areas' of intensive livestock farming are not effective enough.

Conclusions

In recent decades the EU agricultural policy has had considerable spatial impacts in the Netherlands, particularly on dairy farming, beef production and some arable crops (grain, starch potatoes, sugar beet). This influence will decline in the coming years as a result of the further liberalisation of EU agricultural policy, which will be felt most strongly in the dairy farming sector. In the absence of full compensation from the EU, the expected fall in the price of milk – eventually to around 20 per cent less than current prices – can only be

Figure 11. Large-scale land-based agriculture: large-scale arable and dairy farming

Figure 12. Complexes of agroproduction parks, intensive livestock farming and greenhouse horticulture, in which cooperation in the production chain is located in specific areas

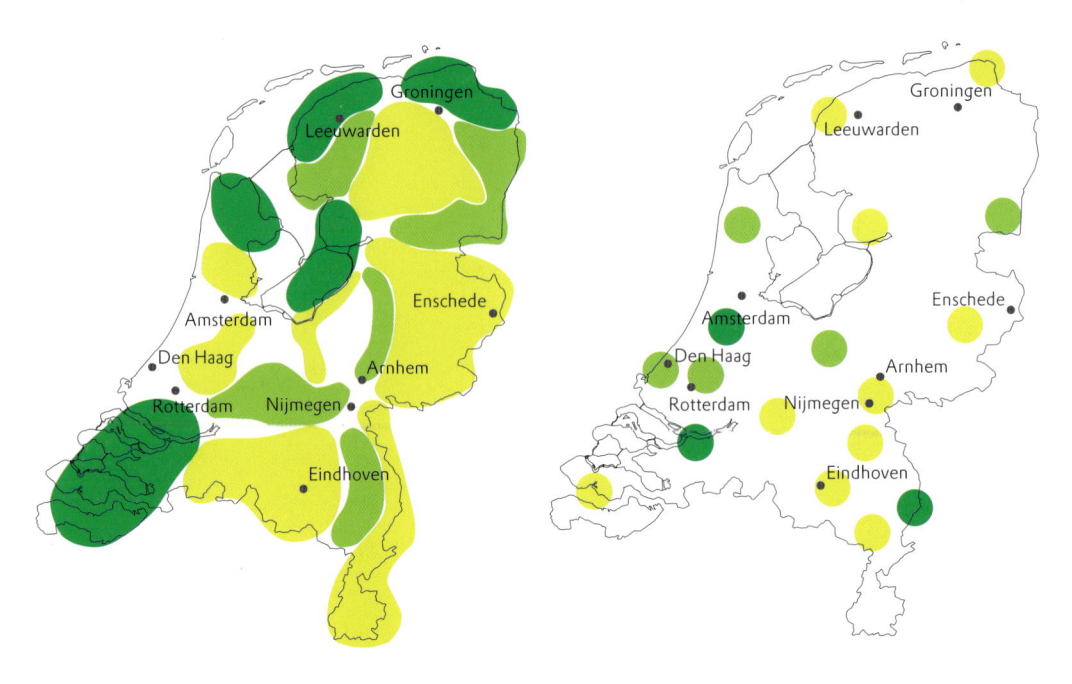

Very good conditions
(good soils, large-scale farmland, relatively little pressure from urban expansion)
– sea clay areas

Good conditions
(soils suitable for grassland, not so large-scale and/or limited pressure from urban expansion)
– river clay areas
– Frisian peat grasslands and low-lying sandy soils
– Veenkoloniën/De Peel

Moderate conditions
(limited areas of good soils, small-scale farm landscape, considerable urban pressure)
– fenland areas
– Gelderse Vallei/northern Veluwe
– Sand soils of Overijssel/Achterhoek
– Sandy soils of Noord-Brabant
– Limburg, except De Peel

Pioneers, international complexes
– Aalsmeer
– Venlo/De Peel
– Moerdijk

National complex
– Westland
– B-triangle/Zuidplaspolder
– Emmen
– Heerhugowaard
– Gelderse Vallei

Regional concentration areas/clusters
– Eemshaven
– Berlikum
– Luttelgeest
– Arnhem-Nijmegen
– Bommelerwaard
– Eindhoven area
– Sloe
– East Nederlands
– De Peel, northern sublocation
– De Peel, southern sublocation

Source: Van Eck et al. (2002: 35)

Source: Van Eck et al. (2002: 38)

UNSEEN EUROPE

Figure 13. 'Amenity agriculture', multifunctional agriculture, based on marketing the amenity aspects of farming (e.g. regional products, on-farm recreation and 'social care farms')

Figure 14. Agri-environmental farming and landscape stewardship, strengthening specific regional cultural, historic, natural and landscape values: the farmer as 'nature entrepreneur'

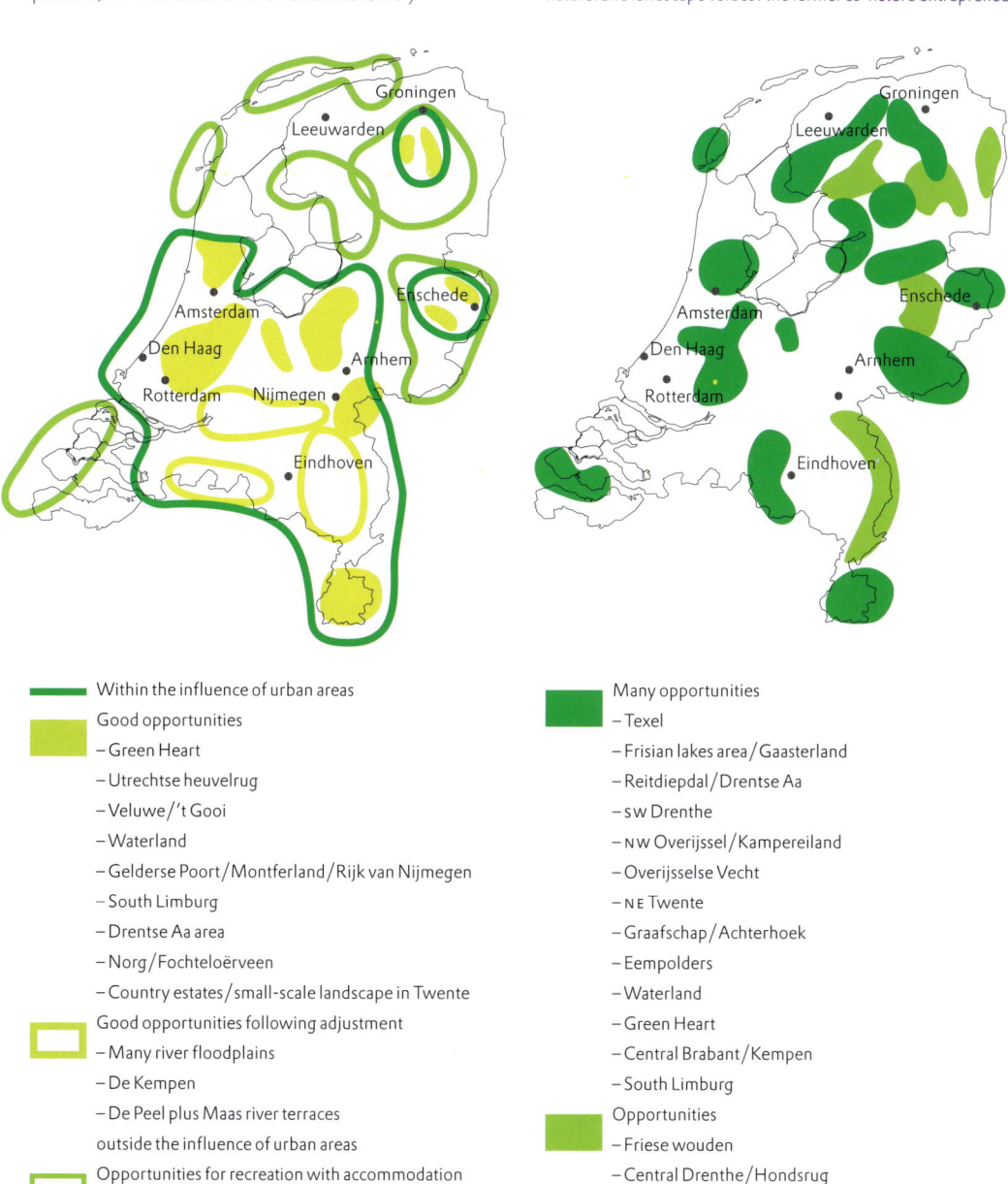

Within the influence of urban areas
Good opportunities
- Green Heart
- Utrechtse heuvelrug
- Veluwe/'t Gooi
- Waterland
- Gelderse Poort/Montferland/Rijk van Nijmegen
- South Limburg
- Drentse Aa area
- Norg/Fochteloërveen
- Country estates/small-scale landscape in Twente

Good opportunities following adjustment
- Many river floodplains
- De Kempen
- De Peel plus Maas river terraces

outside the influence of urban areas
Opportunities for recreation with accommodation
- Texel and other Wadden islands
- Frisian lakes/NW Overijssel
- Drents plateau/Friese wouden
- Twente/Salland/Achterhoek
- Zeeland coast

Many opportunities
- Texel
- Frisian lakes area/Gaasterland
- Reitdiepdal/Drentse Aa
- SW Drenthe
- NW Overijssel/Kampereiland
- Overijsselse Vecht
- NE Twente
- Graafschap/Achterhoek
- Eempolders
- Waterland
- Green Heart
- Central Brabant/Kempen
- South Limburg

Opportunities
- Friese wouden
- Central Drenthe/Hondsrug
- Westerwolde
- Salland
- Walcheren/Zak van Zuid-Beveland

Source: Van Eck et al. (2002: 41)

Source: Van Eck et al. (2002: 44)

Agriculture

absorbed through further intensification and expansion of livestock farming. The other forms of agricultural production in the Netherlands, which are less regulated or are only indirectly influenced by the EU, will also have to undergo a process of intensification, specialisation and expansion to survive further liberalisation and growing global competition. This will affect arable farming and horticulture the most, but also the intensive livestock sector. Relatively high land prices, tough environmental standards and nature conservation regulations, as well as increasing pressures on land for urban growth, habitat management and water storage, will make it difficult to realise the required increase in the scale of production, particularly in the densely populated western part of the country. Rural development policy, in combination with land use planning and water policies – with an injection of increased funding from the EU – can become an important factor in the future development of the countryside (see Chapter 'Spatial policy issues and the EU). This will be most marked in areas under the greatest pressures for urban expansion, where agricultural intensification is more difficult or undesirable, and where extensive forms of farming are unlikely to develop without extra encouragement and assistance.

Further research

As this survey has shown, the impact of the common agricultural policy in the Netherlands is a relatively well-researched topic. Various Dutch research institutes and the Ministry of Agriculture, Nature and Food Quality are currently active in this area. As was the case with regional policy, however, studies on the economic impacts tend to overshadow any geographical analysis. So there remains a paucity of spatial research in this area, making it a potentially fruitful topic for further in-depth research, especially considering the far-reaching reforms now being implemented by the EU. Any further research should take account of ESPON 2.1.3. programme on the spatial impacts of European agriculture policies (the final report is expected in August 2004, but the third interim report can already be obtained from the ESPON website).

Competition policy

COMPETITION POLICY

Introduction

Besides putting an end to war between European nations, the primary motivation for embarking on the European project was to eradicate trade barriers. This was made possible through the creation of an internal market and is enforced by European Union competition policy. Although primarily a matter of the free flow of people, goods and capital, the creation of a common market has produced some tangible effects on physical space as well. Passport checkpoints and customs controls have been dismantled on many of the EU's internal borders, allowing an uninterrupted flow of cars and lorries where once there were immense queues. Most of the spatial impacts of the common market are more indirect, though. The previous chapter has shown how certain modes of agricultural production have become more profitable in an expanded market and how this caused major changes in the nature, function and appearance of the countryside. Similarly, increasing numbers of EU citizens now live and work outside their native country, affecting labour and property markets, and retailers are increasingly expanding outside their home country, bringing with them new shopping styles and formats (e.g. Ikea) and affecting the scale and distribution of retail outlets. Regulation of competition by the EU (e.g. restrictions on state aid, liberalisation of markets and anti-monopoly legislation) can also indirectly affect spatial development patterns by influencing business location decisions. The internal market has a psychological impact as well, especially by transforming mental maps of border regions from peripheral national areas into international crossover zones.

While many of these developments are due wholly or in part to the creation of a common market, competition policy is not the only factor involved. This chapter examines the various ways in which the common market and EU competition policy have affected spatial developments in the Netherlands. Unfortunately, very little has been published on the links between EU competition policy and spatial developments and so, unavoidably, the research is more speculative, and the information more anecdotal, than in other chapters.

EU policy

Current EU policy on the internal market is relatively straightforward: the aim is to ensure fair and open competition between Member States by abolishing protectionism and monopolies (public and private) and by establishing a 'level playing field' for market players. Between 1958 and 1972, under a common customs policy and eradication of internal trade barriers, trade between the participating EEC countries grew three times faster (i.e. nine-fold) than trade with non-participants (European Commission 1999: 6). The common market has since been the main building block of further cooperation between the Member States. The Single European Act, a milestone in European history, was based on the 1985 White Paper *Completing the Internal Market*, which contained over 300 proposals – centring on the free movement of goods, services, capital and labour – to be introduced by the Member States before 1992 to guide the transition to a true common market (Williams 1996: 82). In 1992, the Maastricht Treaty establishing the European Union introduced a requirement on Member States to conduct an economic policy consistent with the premise of an open market and free trade (Article 86). Since then, countless rules have been introduced at the EU level to break down internal barriers to trade (negative integration) and ensure that competition is fair and even within the enlarged market (positive integration; see Scharpf 1999). Specifically, European competition policy has focused on liberalising telecommunications, energy, postal services and air travel and allowed the purchase of cars in other Member States (the last has complicated efforts by some countries to conduct environmental policy via the price mechanism).

What effect has this had on business? In general, an expanded market area and deregulation is accompanied by corporate consolidation. Although this usually leads to price reductions and expanded choice for consumers, it can also have adverse market effects. Supermarket chains, for example, may gain spatial monopolies in an unregulated market by acquiring their competitors. The potential spatial impact is obvious: the company involved can close some of its outlets and still retain its market share. To prevent this from happening, the European Union has also been active in regulating mergers, and in some cases has blocked them (European Commission 2000: 19-22). EU competition policy, therefore, involves both the deregulation and re-regulation of markets in a continual process of fine-tuning the balance of power between economic actors. The liberalisation of markets can also create spatial competition (between cities and regions), putting strategic locations at an advantage and aggravating regional disparities (Committee on Spatial Development 1999: 14). In this sense, EU competition policy is often in direct conflict with EU regional cohesion policy.

Another internal market issue is state aid. Government subsidies to companies are generally considered a form of unfair competition and Article 87 of the EU Treaty forbids any form of public support to businesses that could distort competition and free trade across national borders; Article 88 requires that Member States declare state support measures to the European Commission for approval. To address the patchy implementation of these rules, EU Member States signed an agreement in March 2001 in Stockholm to reduce state aid by 2003. The efforts to monitor and control public-sector support to private enterprise were further institutionalised by the establishment of an aid register, or 'scoreboard' (European Commission 2000: 29). According to the EU scoreboard, the Netherlands gives the second lowest amount of state aid to industry after Britain (Ministerie van BZ 2003: 98-99). Nevertheless, it is one of the few countries that have actually increased state aid, mainly due to increased support to the railways.

The EU has also set rules on public procurement which seek to ensure fair competition between companies for government contracts, especially between Member States.[1] For example, Directive 90/531/EEC on the procurement procedures of entities operating in the water, energy, transport and telecommunications sectors (and subsequently Directive 2001/78/EC on the use of standard forms in the publication of public contract notices) aims to create a transparent international market for utility companies. Directive 93/37/EEC regulates activities, such as the construction of public facilities and infrastructure, that cost more than 6.24 million Euros and Directive 97/52/EC regulates government contracts for services exceeding 249,681 Euros: such contracts have to be issued according to European rules, including standards for publication and translation of tenders and selection criteria (Klinge-van Rooij et al. 2003: 75, 79). Basically, what all this means is that, since the early 1990s, governments in the EU have not been entirely free to decide who they will contract out work to or purchase goods from. After the publication in 1996 of the Green Paper *Public Procurement in the European Union*, the EU embarked on modernising this policy and improving compliance with its provisions. As we shall see, these measures will have consequences for planning practice, particularly when this involves a public-private partnership.

Expectations
Taking the current objectives of the EU as our starting point, we may expect the evolving EU competition policy to have a number of consequences with spatial implications. The first is a further liberalisation of the energy market by dismantling monopolies and opening up national markets to outside competition (European Commission 2002c: 20). The second issue concerns waste disposal. The workings of the internal market (specifically the provisions of Council Regulation No.259/93 on the supervision and control of shipments of waste within, into and out of the European Community) have already led to the further consolidation of waste disposal companies and their expansion into other markets, such as energy and water. Recent measures include harmonisation of specifications, test methods and standards, improvement of market transparency, and measures to stimulate innovation and recycling. It is expected that the liberalisation and realisation of a 'level playing field' in these areas will be completed by 2010 (Ruijgrok and Erbrink 2000: 27). At the same time, several Member States are showing signs of increasing resistance to the ongoing liberalisation, arguing that intervention is justified in sectors serving the public interest (Ministerie van BZ 2003: 96).

The matter of state aid has been included in the Draft Constitution (Article III-56). According to this document, Member States may support businesses only in certain cases: when it serves social policy by supporting individuals (small entrepreneurs); to repair damage, for example resulting from natural disasters; and aid by Germany to its *Neue Länder*. The Draft Constitution also acknowledges that financial support may given to achieve certain worthy policy goals, such as regional cohesion policy, or to preserve cultural heritage, or in cases where other EU interests are apparent and/or when EU permission has been granted.

1. Before such legislation was introduced, only 2% of public contracts were awarded to non-national firms (http://europa.eu.int/scadplus/leg/en/lvb/l22001.htm).

The enlargement will bring far-reaching changes to the internal market. This may be less dramatic a change as some might expect: free trade via trade agreements (Europe Agreements) has already been in place since the fall of the Iron Curtain in 1990, and sectors such as the automobile industry, retail and telecommunications have been quick to take advantage of this. Although the Europe Agreements have provided for free trade between EU Member States and the candidate countries, the internal market also requires that trade regulations be standardised throughout the Union. The incorporation of EU legislation on food quality, intellectual property, consumer protection, contracts and fair trade will further facilitate and accelerate the free flow of goods (CPB 2003: 25). Viewed positively, the number of consumers for Dutch products will increase by 30 per cent (ERAC 2003: 37); viewed negatively, the enlargement will expose the Dutch economy to competition from the candidate countries, notably inexpensive labour. It may also shift the European economic centre of gravity eastwards, inducing companies to relocate their headquarters away from the Netherlands, a trend which will be accelerated if the EU abolishes a particular Dutch corporate tax shelter (see below). This subject, and other aspects related to the spatial effects of competition policy in the Netherlands, will be treated next.

Consequences for the Netherlands

Besides the obvious spatial effect on mobility in border regions, most of the consequences of the EU internal market and competition policy are less direct and hidden from view. Many Dutch citizens are choosing to live or work across the border to take advantage of differences in fiscal systems, or even planning systems (in the case of Flanders). Recently, there has been a surge of interest in purchasing first or second homes in Germany. This has raised the question of the degree to which *housing and spatial planning policies* of the Member States could interfere with the guaranteed freedom of movement of EU citizens. If so, the EU could nullify such policies, which could seriously constrain the ability of Member States to regulate land use. In 1997 this seemed to be on the cards when the European Court of Justice struck down an attempt by Tyrol to introduce a permit system to prevent homes from being used solely for holidays. Recently, real estate agents have suggested to potential buyers that the Dutch 'holiday homes' policy, which prohibits permanent residence of certain dwellings, is in fact in conflict with European law. No evidence for this has materialised though. According to Professor Bart Hessel (University of Utrecht) it is highly unlikely that the EU will take action in this case as spatial planning has been recognised as a justifiable reason for limiting the freedom of movement of persons, especially if the provisions do not discriminate between Dutch and other EU citizens. For the same reason, the Dutch restrictive Green Heart policy is also unlikely to violate current EU internal market legislation.

In contrast, the *liberalisation* and privatisation of various sectors, promoted by the EU, has had large spatial impacts. The opening up of the telecommunications market to competition has not only resulted in lower prices for consumers, but has led each competitor in the mobile telephone market to set up its own network. As a result, there are more antennas on the roofs of buildings and masts in the countryside than if there had been only one provider.

The liberalisation of the energy market has potentially far-reaching consequences for the Netherlands. Directive 1996/92/EC concerning common rules for the internal market in electricity was implemented in 1999 and the operation is expected to be completed in 2004. This directive abolishes exclusive rights, requires unbundling of network activities from generation and supply activities and includes measures for transparency and non-discrimination (European Commission 2002d). The free operation of the market is expected to result in corporate concentration at the European level, and three of the four largest Dutch generators have already been acquired by foreign multinationals (CPB 2003: 62). The most obvious consequence is that locational decisions on where and how to supply energy in the future will involve discussions with internationally operating private companies. The new distribution channels could result in the Netherlands (a net importer of electricity) receiving more energy from nuclear plants in Belgium. The consolidation indirectly brought about by EU competition policy may even lead to another form of false competition: monopoly or oligopoly, thus inviting another round of intervention. Thus far, the price advantages have not materialised, but uncertainty and confusion has – which has worried electricity intensive enterprises, such as greenhouse horticulture firms. At the same time that the EU is promoting the liberalisation of the energy market, it has issued a directive setting a target for renewable electricity consumption in the EU of 22 per cent of total electricity consumption (van Sambeek et al. 2003). Apart from the obvious environmental benefits, this is motivated by a concern that the patchwork of policies currently in place in Member States to promote renewable energy has made the internal market less transparent and may constitute a form of unfair competition. Most of the renewable electricity in Europe will be derived from hydropower, but for obvious topographical reasons the Netherlands will have to concentrate on other sources, such as biomass and wind energy. The ramifications for the Netherlands of meeting this requirement are discussed extensively in the report *Energie is Ruimte* (Gordijn et al. 2003a). The generation of electricity from the incineration of biomass generally entails the cultivation of quick-growing trees. Although this is a very space-consuming form of electricity production, newly forested areas could also perform a recreational and nature function. However, the liberalisation of the waste disposal market after 2005, and the fear that EU competition policy will nullify current Dutch rules regarding the export of waste for incineration, may result in a reduced supply of material (the Netherlands has comparatively strict standards for the burning of waste), thus reducing the viability of biomass as an energy source (Ruijgrok and Erbrink 2000: 32, 39). As far as wind energy is concerned, although the area of land taken up by wind turbines may not be that significant (only about 100 m^2 each), their indirect impact on the environment is much greater in terms of noise pollution, safety issues, shadows and appearance, ruling them out in many areas in the vicinity of homes (Gordijn et al. 2003: 73). The EU has already indicated that it is prepared to introduce fiscal measures assist with the development of an offshore wind park.

Liberalisation in the transport sector has had significant albeit indirect spatial effects as well. Shortly after the semi-privatisation of the Dutch railways, it was announced that unprofitable lines were to be axed from the network unless additional subsidies were granted. The liberalisation of the air travel market will have ramifications for both mobility as well as company location decisions. The 'Single European Sky' seeks to harmonise aviation regulations throughout the EU to improve market transparency and (in the case of environmental regulations) promote a level playing field. Rationalised and standardised rules will also enable a greater volume of air traffic in Europe, with obvious consequences for mobility and the environment. The liberalisation of the air travel market has encouraged the development of regional airports and small budget airlines (interestingly, this contradicts both EU environmental and transport policies). Germany and Belgium are already investing heavily in regional airports near the Dutch border (although Belgium has come into conflict with another aspect of EU competition policy, on state aid, when it attracted Ryanair to its small Charleroi airport). In addition to the encouragement of privatisation, the most important change is the abolition of the 'home carrier' rule, allowing national airlines to depart from any EU hub they wish. The bilateral Open Skies Agreement negotiated between the EU and US will create an even larger internal market – allowing departures from any EU/US hub – and is likely to result in additional corporate consolidation; the KLM/Air France merger is a good example of this. The effect this will have on Schiphol and its surrounding area is the subject of much speculation and debate. One thing seems certain: the advantage that KLM enjoyed over its European rivals from its special arrangement with the US will disappear as a result of EU competition policy. The issue of the future of Schiphol will be returned to in the chapter on 'Spatial policy issues and the EU' in the discussion on mainports.

As stated, one of the most important aspects of EU competition policy is the regulation of *state aid* to businesses (cf. Figure 15). This not only covers monetary transfers like subsidies, but also favourable tax incentives, guarantees, low land prices and even the provision of infrastructure at below market prices. In principle, such practices are considered a form of unfair competition by the European Commission, which has the exclusive right to determine whether state aid is being provided or not. In so doing, the primary concern is not the rationale behind the aid, but its economic effect, although some recent policy developments seem to indicate that this is changing (i.e. the exclusion of 'services in the public interest' from state aid limitations, including regional radio and television, labour dispute mediation, ambulances, energy services and postal services). Just as state aid is broadly defined, so too is the concept of the state, which encompasses not only official government agencies, but also state-owned companies and organisations in which the state holds a controlling interest. To demonstrate compliance with EU competition policy, the

Figure 15. State aid in the EU-15

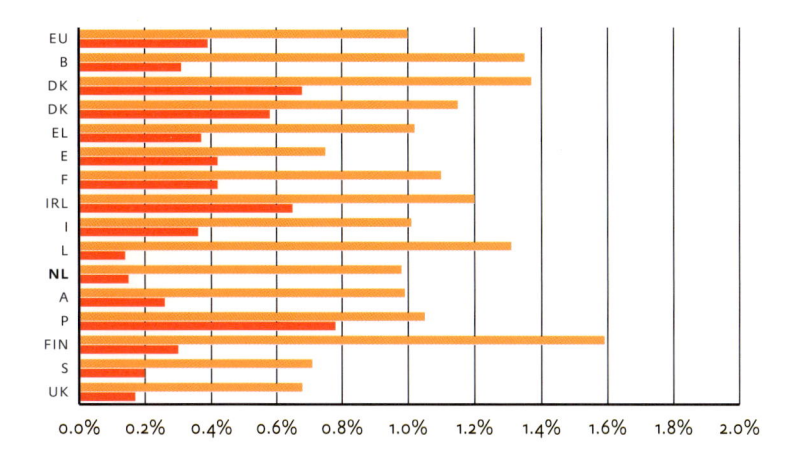

Total aid Total aid less agriculture, fisheries and transport

Source: European Commission (2003c)

Dutch Ministry of the Interior and Kingdom Relations maintains a registry of state aid (*coördinatiepunt staatssteun*) which keeps a record of all the various kinds of support offered to businesses.

European state aid policy can affect spatial developments by interfering with the provision of development incentives. Dutch municipalities have traditionally offered support to businesses to persuade them to settle in their jurisdiction (Klinge-van Rooij 2003:1). Not long ago, for example, the sale of land by the city of Alkmaar to the entrepreneur Dirk Scheringa and the football team AZ resulted in an inquiry by the European Commission. If blocked by the EU, it could have a direct impact on future land use. In many cases, however, there is no EU intervention because the amount of state aid is considered minimal: if a company receives less than 100,000 Euros over a three year period, approval by the European Commission is not required. State aid rules can also complicate the ability of local authorities to become actively involved in the development process by entering into public-private partnerships, which goes against the general trend in planning (and is therefore being contested by the UK, which is accustomed to conducting urban development in this manner). The Dutch urban renewal investment budget (ISV) and similar policies will, therefore, come under the scrutiny of the Commission (Fleurke and Hulst 2002:11). Although permission will probably be granted for urban renewal, incentive packages for small and medium-sized enterprises, environmental clean-up and rural development because these generally correspond with other EU policy areas, EU regulations may create problems for Dutch spatial planning policies which seek to support areas with economic potential (e.g. the mainport strategy). Even in clear cases of regional cohesion, the EU may find public support unacceptable if it believes this is no longer necessary (European Commission 2000:30).

Competition policy

The EU has also intervened to stop government support to Dutch petrol stations near the German border. Because petrol taxes are higher in the Netherlands than in Germany, many Dutch motorists choose to cross the border to refuel. To compensate for this, the Dutch government decided to grant aid to border petrol stations. In so doing, the Dutch authorities considered each station to be a beneficiary as an individual business (although they are in fact subsidiaries of parent companies), and so reasoned that the amount of aid fell short of the EU limit of 100,000 Euros. The European Commission took the opposite view, namely that the parent company was the beneficiary, and in June 2002 demanded that the additional aid be returned (Klinge-van Rooij 2003: 28). If this results in the closure of these petrol stations, this would be a clear spatial consequence of EU competition policy.

Although, as indicated in Figure 15, the Netherlands is second only to the UK in the low levels of direct state aid it provides, there are more hidden forms of aid, such as offering various kinds of tax shelters. Via this route, the Dutch have created a favourable tax climate for international businesses, as described by the International Business Park Friesland:

> One of the great advantages of operating from the Netherlands is its progressive international tax position. It's [sic] flexibility is unequalled in other European countries. From a wide network of tax treaties to the special availability of tax rulings, the Netherlands boasts a robust assortment of factors that will benefit international tax planning ... The Netherlands' long tradition as a trading nation endures as the Dutch government maintains a competitive tax regime which stimulates entrepreneurship and foreign investment in The Netherlands. (www.ibf.nl)

If we are to believe this claim, the imposition of new EU restrictions could have unexpected spatial economic impacts. The tax shelter currently offered by the Dutch Government to parent companies for the foreign earnings of their subsidiaries has recently come under fire from the EU. The existence of this rule may help explain the number of international headquarters located in the Netherlands.[2] The EU is now considering further measures that would prohibit Member States from offering such incentives as part of its wider objective of tackling harmful tax competition in the European Union (Diaw and Gorter 2002).[3] Although this is pure speculation, such rules, if imposed by the EU, may induce mobile capital to relocate, which could have a negatively impact on the office market in countries that had offered incentives.

European directives regulating *public procurement* are designed to ensure that governments buy services according to free market principles, especially when firms from other Member States are involved. The 'Grensmaas' river works project in the province of Limburg serves as an example of how this branch of EU competition policy can interfere with planning. The project involves widening the banks of the Meuse, gravel extraction and stimulating natural processes. Rather than allowing companies to bid for the contract openly, the 450 million Euros contract was simply awarded to a Dutch company that

2. The Dutch are not alone in this: Ireland favours industrial companies and Luxemburg financial ones.

3. Although the authors agree that there are problems with the current situation in which Member States compete for companies by offering tax incentives, the proposed EU rules are likely to make the situation worse. This is because they only apply to measures aimed at attracting and retaining mobile capital; if these are prohibited, countries can be expected to lower their generic corporate tax instead, which will reduce tax revenues.

already owned land along the river banks. A Belgian company subsequently complained to the EU of being excluded from competition, and the Dutch have received a reprimand from Brussels. This conflict has delayed the project significantly. For some time there was a stalemate because the partners indicated that they were not yet ready to tender. A bilateral solution is now being developed in which the project is being subdivided and reallocated between different parties to avoid a tender, but no definite agreement had been reached at the time of writing (spring 2004). One thing is clear, however: even public procurement rules can severely disrupt planning practice.

The precedence given to EU rules can lead to astonishing results. Even in cases where private parties are granted the right by Dutch law to develop their own land (if deemed capable) according to the provisions of the local plan, EU competition policy will override this right to develop if the development in question is commissioned by a public body and exceeds the threshold (Klinge-van Rooij 2003: 75). Since local authorities in such cases are no longer completely free to choose their partners, but must put the work out to tender, this can complicate the establishment of public-private partnerships. Armand Doggen, director of the consultancy centre Aanbestedingen B&U, believes that many changes in practice at the local level will be required to prevent more cases like the Grensmaas project from arising. A recent survey of public institutions in the Netherlands by the consultancy Significant, published in January 2004, found high levels of non-compliance with EU public procurement rules. This was most pronounced at the municipal level, with less than 10 per cent observing EU public procurement rules in 2002.

Finally, although only partly the result of competition policy, we can consider the likely spatial impacts resulting from an enlarged internal market. The enlargement will offer new opportunities for businesses and individuals to relocate to the new Member States, which may affect the property market; some Dutch property investors and developers are quickly expanding their operations into East Europe, as evidenced by a special English-language issue of the Dutch property weekly *Vastgoedmarkt* (30 October 2003). Much of this concerns the purchase of second or holiday homes. There has already been some sign of business relocations, although the evidence for this – for example, Heineken produces beer in Slovakia under the name Zlaty Bazant, and Dutch farmers are emigrating to Eastern Europe, especially Poland – has generally been anecdotal rather than structural in nature (Bruinsma and Hakfort 2004). In addition, growth in trade between the Netherlands and the accession countries is likely to continue: while total Dutch exports slumped in 2002, exports to the 10 accession countries grew by 6 per cent. One of the main industrial sectors likely to be affected by the enlargement is distribution and logistics. It is generally expected that the increased opportunities for Dutch companies outweighs the potential threat of an eastward shift (to Germany, for example). We return to this issue, as it relates to seaports, in the discussion of mainports in the chapter on 'Spatial policy issues and the EU'.

Conclusions

Although there are few directly visible impacts, and although many effects of policy are difficult or impossible to measure, EU internal market and competition policy has a potentially large – if often invisible – indirect influence on spatial development in the Netherlands. This chapter has raised a number of interesting points rarely considered by planners:
- business location decisions are influenced by the opening up of new markets (liberalisation) and regulation of competition
- individual behaviour (living/working abroad) is influenced by the internal market
- government capacity for conducting economic, environmental and spatial policy and for implementing spatial investment projects is affected by state aid restrictions, and planning processes can be affected by public procurement regulations.

Further research
More research is badly needed to illuminate the fascinating but complex relationship between EU competition policy and spatial developments. Thus far, it is the most 'unseen' of the policy areas included in this study. Although there is at present only scant information to build upon, and what is available is scattered across a variety of disciplines, this is an opportunity to engage in pioneering multidisciplinary research.

Environment and Nature

ENVIRONMENT AND NATURE

Introduction

Arguably the most spatially relevant policy area included in this survey – certainly in terms of media attention – is EU environmental policy. Unlike Dutch policies, EU nature and environmental policies are closely integrated (forming in fact one policy field) and will therefore be taken together in our analysis. The measures taken on the basis of these policies sometimes deliver direct and intended effects – such as the designation of protected habitat areas, where certain spatial interventions are prohibited – but most European directives have an indirect impact because their effects depend strongly on the local situation. For example, compliance with the EU's air quality standards can complicate plans for homes within a short distance from motorways. In a densely populated country like the Netherlands, with a high level of personal mobility, and with the highest concentration of people and farm animals per hectare in Europe, environmental and nature standards have a far greater impact than in other Member States. Moreover, the emphasis placed on sustainable development at the EU level will reverberate in countless plans and projects (particularly when EU funding is sought) administered by lower tiers of government.

The purpose of this chapter is to explore how much effect European nature and environmental policies have on spatial developments in the Netherlands. According to the *Environmental Balance 2003* about 80 per cent of Dutch environmental policies originate in 'Brussels' and the EU's influence on all aspects of Dutch environmental policy will increase further (Milieu- en Natuurplanbureau 2003a: 122-125). For this reason, it is understandable to first take a good look at how environmental policy is formulated at the European level.

EU policy

Environmental policy at the EU level finds its justification in the philosophy behind the single common market: competing companies should be able to operate in similar environmental conditions and be subject to the same environmental standards. European policies are further justified by the inherently international nature of many environmental problems. This is reflected in the broadening scope of European environmental policy over the years, starting with local industrial pollution control and emission and noise standards for cars in the 1970s to regional problems, such as acidification of forests and water pollution, in the 1980s, and finally, in the 1990s, the recognition by the EU of global environmental issues (greenhouse gases, climate change). The importance of environmental policy is also apparent in the Treaty of Maastricht (1992), which states that environmental protection should become integrated into all other policy sectors of the EU. This principle has been given concrete form in the obligation on Member States to introduce a system of environmental impact assessment (EIA) for certain public and private projects (Directive 85/337/EEC and Directive 97/11/EC). Where spatial plans and proposed construction projects are likely to have significant impacts on the environment or nature, these should be investigated properly beforehand, their anticipated effects made clear to the public and, where possible, taken into account in the decision-making process. This was taken a step further when the Gothenburg European Council (2001) agreed that implementation of the EU Sustainable Development Strategy will be a key goal of environmental policy. An annual environmental policy review of progress with environmental policy integration at the Member State level and for the EU as a whole is being monitored in the 'Cardiff process', starting with the spring 2004 report (European Commission 2003e). These measures are intended to ensure that sustainable development is a standard consideration in all of the sectoral policies of the EU. They introduce an extra dimension into all spatially relevant policy instruments, such as support schemes under agricultural, transport and regional policy, and have to be taken into account by applicants and planning authorities.

The Birds Directive (Council Directive 79/409/EEC), adopted in 1979, was the first piece of EU legislation on nature policy to have a direct effect on land use in protection areas designated by the Member States, and even outside these areas. Similarly, the Habitats Directive (Council Directive 92/43/EEC) aims to conserve biological diversity, specifically the most important endangered plant and animal species, and consequently covers much larger areas. Both the Birds Directive and the Habitats Directive have, in essence, two main goals: the conservation of endangered species, for which the Member States have to introduce appropriate measures (to prevent the capture of wild animals, the collection of wild plants and disturbance to animals and habitats, and carrying out targeted habitat and landscape management); and to ensure that physical interventions (e.g. the construction of roads and industrial estates) do not damage the habitats of certain endangered plant and animal species. To this end, the Member States have to identify protection areas and submit the details to the European Commission, which then assesses these against the requirements in the two directives. After the Commission has approved the proposed list of protected areas, the Member States have to formally designate them. Eventually, all these protected areas should together function as a European ecological network: Natura 2000.

The European Commission has critically followed the incorporation of these regulations into national law (in letter and in spirit) and many countries have had considerable difficulties in this process, particularly when it comes to the designation of protected areas.[1] These directives have been of great administrative and symbolic significance because decisions by the European Court of Justice and national case law have made it clear that in certain cases decisions on spatial developments can be tested for compliance directly against the

1. The Netherlands was not immune to this: it received two instructions from the Commission on its proposed list of protected areas under the Birds and Habitats Directives. The European Court of Justice has even ruled against Ireland because it had taken insufficient protection measures for a particular species, quite apart from its obligation to designate protected areas.

directives – certainly as long as their incorporation into national law is not yet complete (Freriks et al. 2002). Transposition of the Habitats and Birds Directives into national law is also expected to place considerable demands on the ten new Member States over the next few years. This will involve not only overcoming public resistance to restrictions on land use in the interests of European nature policy, but also amending the existing EU lists of protected species and habitats. The 'green lobby' expects that the new Member States, besides asking for a postponement, will probably make a case for changing EU nature policy. Another development in nature policy that could have significant spatial implications is the intention of the environment ministers of the North Sea countries, expressed at the North Sea Conference in Bremen (25 June 2003), to draw up an inventory of vulnerable nature protection areas in the North Sea before 2006. Important natural values in these areas (which include five areas within the exclusive economic zone of the Netherlands) are threatened by intensive fishing practices and water pollution. This designation could directly conflict with plans to build more wind turbines on the North Sea.

Consequences for the Netherlands

It is not easy to measure with complete accuracy what spatial effects European directives will actually have. For the directives in the field of nature policy this will eventually become clear from the designated protection areas (and maps), but the situation is far from clear for the environmental directives. An important principle of environmental policy is controlling pollution at the source (per vehicle, factory or substance), although, of course, in the end the object is to prevent harmful effects on people and nature. EU directives are seldom formulated so that at a certain distance from the source they impose direct restrictions on land use (immission standards). In short, the spatial implications of EU legislation in practice depend to a great extent on national implementation, the local situation and especially on the nature and scale of the source.

Nature
In the Netherlands the basic structure for implementing the Habitats Directive – the National Ecological Network – has already been established by central government in various spatial and other policy plans, including the National Structure Plan for the Rural Areas (*Structuurschema Groene ruimte*) and the Fifth National Policy Document on Spatial Planning (*Vijfde nota over de Ruimtelijke Ordening*) and the spatial planning key decision on the Wadden Sea (*Planologische Kernbeslissing Waddenzee*).

As stated, the Birds Directive aims to protect all wild birds found in the EU and their habitats. Under its provisions, the Member States, among other actions, have to designate Special Protection Areas, which include water areas of international significance. For this reason, a large number of protection areas under the Birds Directive can also be recognised as wetlands of international importance under the Ramsar Convention. At the moment in the Netherlands there are 79 Special Protection Areas under the Birds Directive and their protection is linked to the relevant provisions of the Habitats Directive (article 7). The implementation of these directives requires not only the designation of the areas that contain the species and habitats to be protected, but also the amendment of national regulations pertinent to the management and prevention measures. An Order in Council has been issued for this purpose, based on article 29 of the Nature Protection Act 1998. This states that decisions on the implementation of plans and projects in the designated protection areas are subject to the assessment framework in the Habitats Directive. The planning protection will be based mainly on the Nature Protection Act 1998; a proposed amendment to the Act relating to this directive is still before Parliament waiting for a reading. Until this becomes law, the Habitats Directive may in many cases be directly applicable (article 6(2)) when changing the zoning of land within a protection area if this could lead to a deterioration of natural habitats (Freriks et al. 2002: 53). This can even apply to possible developments outside these areas that may endanger the survival of the species or the maintenance of their habitats. The essence of the obligations relating to building plans can be summarised in five steps:

1. screening
2. assessment of significant impacts (including those outside the protection areas)
3. examination of alternatives
4. determination of imperative reasons of overriding public interest
5. compensatory measures.

All these steps must be taken and any compensatory measures required must be operational before the relevant administrative body can give formal approval for the proposed activity (article 6(3,4) of the Habitats Directive). In addition, the Member State must inform the European Commission of the compensatory measures adopted.

At the beginning of 2003 the Netherlands submitted a list of 141 sites for designation under the Habitats Directive to the European Commission; these were approved on 8 July 2003. This made the Netherlands the first country in the European Union to formally fulfil this obligation and make its contribution to Natura 2000 – although amendments to the Nature Protection Act will be needed for a good management and effective protection of these areas. The total area of the Dutch Habitats Directive sites is 750,841 ha (see Figure 16).

The EU had already been notified about the majority of these protection areas in 1998. Of the total area, 70,545 ha represents an extension of previously identified sites and 24,836 ha are new sites; a further 48,965 ha can be discounted because the ecological conditions and opportunities in these areas have already deteriorated. The extended areas are mostly water bodies under central government management, with the addition of the navigation channels in the Wadden Sea, the North Sea coastal zone and the Westerschelde. The Veluwe site has been extended to include the military training areas. The new sites are mainly areas of characteristic Dutch habitats and species, such as wet heaths and fen meadows, and habitats of species such as the Northern or Root Vole. These Dutch habitats are highly important from a European point of

Figure 16. Natura 2000 conservation areas in the Netherlands

Source: Expertisecentrum LNV

view; of the 198 'natural habitat types of community interest' identified by the EU, 51 are found in the Netherlands, almost as many as the United Kingdom, a much larger and, in many people's eyes, more 'natural' country (Janssen and Schaminée 2003). Of the protection areas designated under the Habitats Directive, 640,086 ha overlap with areas protected under the Birds Directive: more than 95 per cent of the protected areas of national water bodies and about 75 per cent of the terrestrial areas. We should also bear in mind that in the future, these areas may be adjusted according to the presence (or absence) of a designated bird and/or other species. Moreover, it is important that the compulsory protection against construction and other detrimental effects extends beyond the boundaries of the protected areas, the key consideration being whether the plan or activity under consideration can have 'significant effects' on the protected species or habitats. One example is a water level ordinance that regulates the water level in an adjoining area; another is the presence of intensive livestock farms near a protected area. Regarding the latter, a zoning system under the manure and ammonia policy was presented to the lower house of Parliament on 11 September 2003. This proposes zones of 500 and 1500 metres around the protected areas designated under the Habitats and Birds Directives, within which extra restrictions will apply to existing and new intensive livestock farms.

The spatial significance of the regulation for large construction projects was highlighted by the recent decision by the Council of State to annul a decision by the Zeeland provincial executive that would have formed the land-use planning framework for the construction of the Westerschelde Container terminal near Vlissingen. An important consideration was that insufficient account was taken of the Habitats and Birds Directives during the preparation of the plans.

In response to complaints (e.g. Didde 2000), mainly from the business community, about difficulties arising from the implementation of these directives, an Interdepartmental Policy Study (*Interdepartementaal beleidsonderzoek*) was conducted and the results and the Government's conclusions were recently presented to Parliament. The study establishes that there is considerable public support for improving the implementation of these directives, while remaining true to their objectives, through better provision of information, clear policy decisions and further research, particularly into the national distribution of protected plant and animal species. The Government has adopted most of the recommendations with the aim of making the implementation of the directives more effective.

Environment
The spatial effects of European environmental policy are due in part to standards contained in European directives, for example on water and air quality, which may prohibit certain construction and other activities if these exceed any limit values. Environmental policy will also have spatial effects through the 'external integration' policies, which work with instruments to ensure that, where relevant, environmental policies are incorporated into other sectors.

External integration
Environmental impact assessment (EIA) has proved to be an important tool in spatial planning: the aim is to ensure that environmental and nature protection objectives are applied to certain projects with a spatial dimension by obliging the project proponent to assess the impacts on nature and the environment, consider possible alternatives and make the findings public. The relevant public authority must take any possible impacts fully into account and explain its final decision. The EIA Directive (97/11/EEC) has now been extended to include strategic environmental assessment (SIA) with the adoption of Directive 2001/42/EC on the assessment of the effects of certain plans and programmes on the environment. This directive extends the obligation to conduct an environmental assessment to almost all government plans with a spatial dimension, from local land use plans to the more strategic plans made by the provinces and central government. The EIA regulations initially caused considerable problems in the Netherlands because of the link to spatial planning processes, but are now accepted as a normal part of the planning system. Nevertheless, incorporation of the new SEA directive into Dutch law is proving to be not so simple. The directive must be incorporated into national legislation by 21 July 2004, but the draft legislation has not yet been put before Parliament (January 2004).

The Sixth Environmental Action Programme 2001–2010 (European Commission 2001d) also sets out a number of 'horizontal integration' measures as part of the external integration policy, including:
- dissemination of best practices on sustainable spatial planning
- the *Green Paper on Urban Transport*, the Sustainable Cities and Towns Network, and the Demonstration Programme on Integrated Coastal Zone Management
- promoting environmentally friendly land management through amendments to the EU agricultural policy and cohesion policy (regional funds).

Climate and energy
Another priority of EU environmental policy is to stabilise the concentration of greenhouse gases in the atmosphere (implementation of the Kyoto Protocol). This entails realising an 8 per cent reduction in greenhouse gases in 2008–2012 compared with the 1990 level. The EU has announced the introduction of various measures, for example in urban planning, agriculture and infrastructure, to combat the adverse effects of climate change. These have not yet been developed to a stage where spatial effects can be predicted. Meanwhile, a consensus has emerged on the expected changes to the climate: besides a rise in sea levels of 9–88 cm by the end of this century, Europe will have to prepare itself for more frequent heatwaves and extreme precipitation events; the whole of Europe will become warmer, Northern Europe wetter and Southern Europe drier (Ministerie van VROM 2001a: 32).

With regard to the environmental policy/energy nexus, the main spatially relevant aspects are the proposals on renewable energy, agriculture and forestry for reducing emissions of nitrogen oxides and methane, and a proposed underground storage facility for CO_2. The EU seeks to increase the proportion of energy generated from renewable sources from 14 per cent in 1997 to 22.1 per cent in 2010. The relevant directive contains indicative targets for each Member State, based on their geographic and climatic characteristics.[2] The Netherlands faces a considerable challenge in meeting its target because it is making slow progress with the introduction of renewable electricity (see Table 8). A recent study by Energy Research Centre of the Netherlands (ECN) contains a comparison of the various national policy instruments within the EU used to encourage the introduction of renewable electricity. The Dutch demand-side approach (ecotax) forms an exception to the general trend and appears to heavily support imports of renewable electricity from surrounding countries. Most of the other countries work with compensations for returned energy and compulsory purchase by producers or consumers of a certain percentage of renewable electricity (Sambeek et al. 2003). If the Netherlands were to switch to some sort of compulsory system, domestic production of renewable energy would probably increase rapidly, biomass and wind energy being the main options. Denmark, which has similar wind conditions, generates about four times as much wind energy as the Netherlands (2900 MW compared with 700 MW). The best opportunity for increasing the generation of renewable energy in the Netherlands is developing wind parks in the North

2. Directive 2001/77/EC of the European Parliament and of the Council of 27 September 2001 on the promotion of electricity produced from renewable energy sources in the internal electricity market.

Table 8. Targets for renewable electricity in the EU-15

	Production of electricity from renewable sources in 2000 (per cent)					Tentative targets for 2010
	Hydro	Wind	Biomass	Geothermal	Total	
B	0.5	0.0	1.1	0.0	1.6	6.0
UK	1.4	0.3	1.2	0.0	2.8	10.0
NL	0.2	0.9	3.6	0.0	4.7	9.0
IRL	3.5	1.0	0.4	1.7	4.9	13.2
D	4.1	1.6	1.1	0.0	6.8	12.5
EL	6.9	0.8	0.0	0.0	7.7	20.1
F	12.5	0.0	0.6	0.0	13.1	21.0
E	13.1	2.1	1.0	0.0	16.2	29.4
DK	0.1	12.3	4.8	0.0	17.2	29.0
L	10.2	2.3	4.8	0.0	17.3	5.7
I	16.0	0.2	0.7	0.0	18.6	25.0
P	25.9	0.4	3.5	0.0	30.0	39.0
FIN	20.9	0.1	12.2	0.0	33.3	31.5
S	54.1	0.3	2.7	0.0	57.1	60.0
A	67.3	0.1	2.6	0.2	70.0	78.1
EU	12.4	0.9	1.5	0.2	14.9	22.0

Source: Directive 2001/77/EC

Sea, although as indicated before, this could eventually come into conflict with EU nature policy.[3] The previous chapter contains a brief explanation of the implications of the competition policy for the energy market.

Local environmental quality
A third theme in European environmental and nature policy with important spatial effects is the local environmental quality cluster: air pollution, safety and nuisance. In this area the EU has a long tradition of research, policymaking and setting standards. The main instruments are enhanced environmental quality standards (to improve public health), product standards, integrated prevention and control of industrial installations and national emission ceilings (Clean Air For Europe, CAFE programme). The programme includes a review of the effectiveness of all EU legislation relating to air quality. Of direct spatial relevance is the Air Quality Framework Directive (1996/62/EC), particularly the tightening of air pollution policy relating to nitrogen oxides and particulates (fine particles and dust in the air), which can lead to restrictions on new building near busy roads (Klinge-van Rooij 2003: 188).[4] In the Netherlands the Air Quality Framework Directive, and its three daughter directives for sulphur dioxide, nitrogen oxides, nitrogen dioxide, fine particulates and lead, has been implemented by the Air Quality Decree. The formal national emission inventory required by the EU for the year 2002 gives a good indication of the spatial distribution of air quality problems. The only limit values exceeded are those for nitrogen dioxide: about 300,000 people are exposed to higher concentrations of nitrogen dioxide than permitted by the EU directive, and the 2010 limit value for particulates (PM10) is exceeded throughout almost the

3. These are described in more detail in the Netherlands Institute for Spatial Research's report *Energie is Ruimte* (Gordijn et al. 2003a); an English summary is available on our website: www.ruimtelijkplanbureau.nl).
4. Council Directive 1999/30/EC of 22 April 1999 relating to limit values for sulphur dioxide, nitrogen dioxide and oxides of nitrogen, particulate matter and lead in ambient air.

entire country. The *Environmental Balance 2003* mentions that 3,000 to 30,000 people in the Netherlands living in central urban areas and near busy motorways will probably be exposed to higher than permitted concentrations of nitrogen dioxides in 2010 (Milieu- en Natuurplanbureau 2003a). Neither will the concentrations of particulates (PM10) be brought within the EU (daily) limit values for 2005. The Dutch Environmental Assessment Agency does expect that source-directed measures will reduce air pollution over the coming years, although local hot spots near busy motorways and in urban centres will remain (Milieu- en Natuurplanbureau 2003a: 28). Uncertainties have also arisen in 'pipeline plans' (previously approved developments) and 'transitional situations' about the translation of air quality standards into spatial zones for the construction of new houses or other 'sensitive facilities' (schools, hospitals, sports fields) near roads where the limit values are exceeded. The implementation of this directive has led to delays and restrictions on a number of house-building schemes on sites near motorways, including projects in Breda, Barendrecht and Schiedam. In Maastricht the ambient concentrations of particulates are so high that, strictly speaking, no new building should be permitted at all. For the moment, the city council does not intend to stop all building projects and has notified the Ministry of Spatial Planning, Housing and the environment of the problem.

The Dutch Government fears that enhanced emission standards for industrial activities and cars will not have the desired effects soon enough, and has taken steps to convince the European Commission to introduce extra source-directed measures. It has also asked for an extension to the period within which the specified NO_2 limit values have to be met (2015 instead of 2010); in 2000 it had previously notified the Commission of the impossibility of meeting the standards for particulates. The European Commission will consider this in its current review of Directive 1999/30/EC, which sets limit values for nitrogen oxides and particulate matter in ambient air. National environmental policy is intended primarily to ensure that EU NO_2 limit values for 2010 are met in new situations (new roads, new building near busy roads and urban renewal projects). In practice, this prohibits building near busy main roads, in the most heavily affected areas to about 150 metres from the motorway, or requires converting the relevant stretch of the motorway into an underpass (Ministerie van VROM 2002: 27). The Air Quality Decree legislates directly for the implementation of EU standards in town planning: the relevant administrative bodies 'when exercising powers that may have consequences for air quality...take account of the following limit values...' (in articles 5, 8, 12, 13, 15-17 of the Air Quality Decree). One implication of this is that when adopting regional or local plans and issuing permits under article 19 of the Spatial Planning Act (planning permission in anticipation of a revision of the local land use plan), land may not be zoned for new housing, other sensitive uses, roads or industrial and commercial premises if this would lead to exceedance of a limit value. This puts great pressure on the research required during the preparation of spatial plans. These studies must take account of a gradual reduction in air pollution along roads resulting from source-directed measures (including environmental licences and tightening emission standards for cars), despite the expected increase in the numbers of sources (road traffic) compared with the reference year (2010), and estimates must be made of the influence of local sources in relation to the background level and diffuse sources of pollution. Interesting legal questions could arise with respect to plans for the construction of new homes if, despite the fact that the limit value would be exceeded, a local authority grants permission because the relevant land use plan has not been updated to include the provisions of the Air Quality Decree. In such cases, the courts would most likely order a moratorium on construction. To avoid this, the provincial and municipal authorities will have to prepare a good inventory of the (potential) problem areas, with maps that indicate such 'risk zones'. Subsidies are now available to allow the municipalities and provinces to draw up the required air quality plans based on these inventories.

At the end of 2003 the Dutch Government had to submit its second formal report on air quality in the Netherlands to the European Commission. This will include reports by the municipal and provincial authorities. Based on their own inventories, the municipalities must draw up action plans for resolving the identified exceedances of air quality limit values before 1 May 2004 (Air Quality Decree). Only then will there be a reliable picture of the local problem areas and possible spatial measures to resolve these (such as limits on house building, demolition/redevelopment plans, road realignment and traffic control measures). The largest Dutch cities have chosen to adopt effect-oriented traffic management measures and introduce cleaner buses, closing city centres to traffic and the designation of 'low emission zones' (see Chapter 'Spatial policy issues and the EU' of this report and www.london-lez.org).

The Netherlands Environmental Assessment Agency recently published a study of the potential problem areas along motorways (not in city centres), which indicates that the relevant EU limit values are likely to be exceeded in 2010 (the benchmark year for this directive) along a distance of 120-220 km of motorway (Blom et al 2003). This affects about 100 to 3000 dwellings (see Table 9). A preliminary conclusion is that for some years to come this directive will have considerable consequences for the construction of new homes in the direct vicinity of busy roads in city centres and along some stretches of motorway, particularly around Amsterdam and Rotterdam.

Another EU directive with important spatial consequences in the Netherlands is the 'IPPC Directive' (1996/61/EC) on Integrated Pollution Prevention and Control, which, in combination with the prescribed national emission ceiling for ammonia (NEC Directive, 2000/81/EC), requires the designation of vulnerable nature conservation areas. In the Netherlands, the main source of ammonia emissions are intensive livestock units. In their letter to the lower house of Parliament, dated 11 September 2003, the State Secretary for the Environment (VROM) and the Minster of Agriculture (LNV) link this to the protected areas under the Habitats and Birds Directives. As a result, no new intensive livestock units are permitted in a 500 metre zone around these protected areas and expansion of existing farms is (almost entirely) prohibited. At a distance of 1500 metres, ammonia emissions from existing and new farms

Figure 17. Homes within NO$_2$ exceedance zones along motorways in 2015

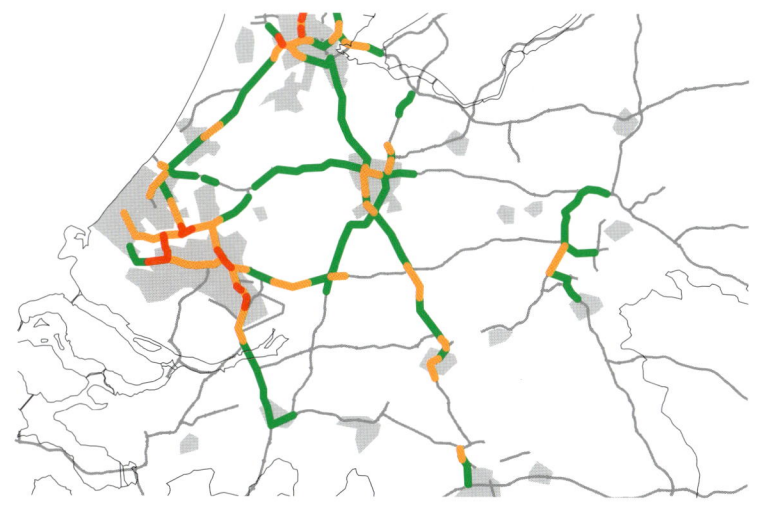

Almost certainly no homes within exceedance areas
Some homes may be in exceedance areas
The 15 sections of motorway with the highest number of homes in exceedance areas

Source: Blom et al. (2003: 11)

Table 9. Development of NO$_2$ levels near motorways

Trend in NO$_2$ concentrations along motorways	2001	2010	2015
NO$_2$ total (mg/m3)	55	38-41	36-39
NO$_2$ background (mg/m3)	37	26-29	25-28
NO$_2$ emissions from road (mg/m3)	20	13	12-13
Number of homes in exceedance area	>300,000	100-3000	15-1500
Km motorway with exceedance at 25m	500	120-220	90-160

Source: Blom et al. (2003: 9)

will be subject to a ceiling of 2000 kg per farm. This regulation is having a direct effect on the restructuring plans the provinces of Gelderland, Overijssel, Noord-Brabant and Limburg have to make under the Restructuring of the Concentration Areas Act (van Buuren 2003). These plans must translate the provisions of the EU directives into new zones that define restrictions on building for the relevant farms.

Safety
In 1982 the EU adopted the 'Seveso Directive' to limit the risks of serious accidents at certain industrial plants. This has now been replaced by the 1992 Seveso 2 Directive (96/82/EC), which has been largely implemented in the Netherlands by the Hazards of Major Accidents Decree 1999. This applies to

almost 300 large industrial installations, mostly located on industrial estates, for which the safety zones cover a total of about 8300 ha (10-6 contour) (Milieu- en Natuurplanbureau 2003b). The transposition of the spatial aspect of this directive (article 12) into Dutch law has not yet been approved and adopted, but a draft decree on external safety standards for industrial installations was published in 2002. This contains provisions for safety zones around hazardous industrial installations to protect vulnerable objects such as homes. When granting environmental licences to the companies concerned and when adopting land use plans within the defined safety zones, competent authorities must take account of the limit values contained in this decree. A number of provincial councils have already drawn up risk maps showing the main areas and roads potentially affected by safety risks (besides the 'Seveso installations', these include LPG tanks, firework storage depots, transportation routes for hazardous substances, etc.). This can be considered as an impact on spatial developments in so far as these EU directives may have initiated Dutch actions to separate potentially hazardous installations from new housing, schools and the like.

Noise pollution
Directive 2002/49/EC relating to the assessment and management of environmental noise covers all important sources of noise to which humans are exposed (road, rail, industry and aircraft noise). There will be no central EU standards (limit values) set. Instead each Member State must prepare strategic noise maps and draw up action plans of measures to manage noise and its effects; specific measures to be taken are at the discretion of the municipal and provincial councils in their action plans. Not only homes but also 'quiet areas in open country' and quiet areas in agglomerations, such as public parks and courtyard gardens, must be included in the noise maps. The noise maps and action plans to combat the greatest disturbances caused by noise to be used for the implementation of this law must be prepared in 2007 and 2008 respectively.

This directive must be transposed into national legislation by 18 July 2004 at the latest. A bill to incorporate the provisions of the directive into existing legislation, such as the Noise Abatement Act, was put before the lower house of Parliament on 2 September 2003. This bill states that the new noise indicator will not yet be used in the standards (maximum allowable noise annoyance levels). However, the recently amended Aviation Act, which contains provisions for Schiphol Airport, includes the noise indicator from the directive. The Council of State invoked the new noise indicator for overall annoyance (Lden) in its recent rejection of the proposed extension to the runway at Eelde airport because this is better at predicting the real noise annoyance than the current Ke method. Nevertheless, it is expected that the direct spatial consequences of this directive in the Netherlands will not be very great because the Noise Abatement Act already goes further than similar legislation in other countries. The noise maps, though, may provide a new impetus at the local level for tackling certain persistent noise problems (particularly if they coincide with excessive air pollution levels), while the use of the new noise indicators may lead to a new public debate on the noise zoning around Schiphol Airport and the regional airports (Koppert 2001).

Conclusions

We can draw five main conclusions from our survey of the spatial impacts of EU nature and environmental policies:
- The direct consequences of European nature policy (Habitats and Birds Directives) are obvious and considerable (affecting 750,000 ha); the spatial effects of European environmental policy are much narrower in scope, although not yet fully in the picture.
- The difference in approach to nature and environmental policy taken by the Netherlands and the EU is striking. While the Netherlands thinks more in terms of goals, target values and guidance values, the EU sets strict limit values and area designations which are directly enforceable (as an obligation to produce results) via the Dutch courts or European Court of Justice.
- In time, air pollution and noise abatement policies in particular can impose local restrictions on urban building projects and the planning of new roads.
- The need to incorporate European environmental and nature conservation regulations into spatial and land use plans makes great demands on the plan preparation process, including the identification of all possible problem areas, because these regulations are found mainly in sectoral legislation (not planning law).
- The construction of wind parks at sea may receive a further stimulus as a result of European climate policy (or extra pressure on the Netherlands to achieve its targets for renewable electricity).

Further research
The impact of EU environmental policy (which includes nature) on spatial developments has great potential for further in-depth research. Curiously, there is no ESPON study underway that examines the territorial effects of environmental policy in the Member States. However, quite a lot of work is already available on the implementation of EU environmental legislation in the Netherlands, and any in-depth study will need to build upon this. Specific research topics include:
- Mapping the exact spatial effects of EU environmental/nature policy in the Netherlands, and contrasting this with plans for urbanisation and infrastructure development.
- Researching the most effective manner to implement EU environmental/nature regulations (i.e. sectoral, via the planning system or both).
- Comparing the implementation and administration of EU environmental/nature policy in the Netherlands with other Member States.
- Evaluating the claim that the Netherlands is indeed a special case when it comes to environmental rules (due to its population density, intensive agriculture, location in Europe and high mobility).

Water

Introduction

In December 2003 a number of Dutch newspapers carried an article on the results of a study by the research institute Alterra. The conclusions could not have been starker: implementation of the Water Framework Directive would result in the loss of more than half of all the land-based agricultural production in the Netherlands (Van der Bolt et al. 2003). But the researchers reserve judgement on their findings, though, and the politicians do not expect that things will be as bad as they are made out to be. Nevertheless, European water legislation may have a significant influence on Dutch spatial planning. The existence of European legislation means that the Netherlands does not have full control over water policy. Because the Netherlands lies in the delta of the rivers Rhine, Meuse, Scheldt and Eems, the water quality of the surface waters and the safety of homes and businesses in the river floodplains depend to a certain extent on activities in other countries further upstream. Potential solutions to the problems that arise also fall outside the scope of Dutch regulations.

This chapter looks at the European agreements and directives relevant to water management and the spatial effects they can be expected to have. The first part of the chapter examines European policy in the field of water, both in terms of regulations and subsidies; the second part looks at the impact of these on spatial developments in the Netherlands.

EU policy

The problems of flooding and safety are being tackled under agreements and treaties between individual Member States and are not directly covered by EU policy. The European Commission is also looking into the issue of flooding. Whether this will lead to a directive on flood prevention is highly questionable because a large number of countries have not yet indicated their willingness to support the idea. At the moment the problems associated with water quantity are only being addressed in bilateral agreements and within the EU via subsidised Interreg projects (see section 'Consequences for the Netherlands' in the Chapter 'Regional policy'). The implementation of many of these Interreg water projects is being managed by international commissions; the most important of these are described in this chapter. The agreements are made between individual Member States in varying coalitions and so they do not have that status of EU directives. Nevertheless, recipients of EU subsidies must meet the relevant policy criteria, in effect an indirect way of pursuing policy. Because these EU-funded agreements can have certain effects on physical space (through the restoration of old river meanders, restructuring of

River basins in the Netherlands

The Rhine river basin

The objectives of the majority of the short-term Interreg IIC projects are to limit damage from flooding and reduce safety risks in the floodplain of the Rhine. These projects were implemented under the Interreg IIC Rhine Meuse Activities (IRMA) umbrella programme (completed in 2003).

A convention was already in existence for the Rhine, and the International Commission for the Protection of the Rhine against Pollution (ICPRP) has been active for some time. The Netherlands, Germany, Luxembourg, France and Switzerland are parties to this agreement. As in the case of the Meuse, the main channel of the Rhine was initially the subject of protection, the tributaries being included if they were important for the chemical or ecological quality of the main channel. Flooding, ecological restoration and groundwater were added to the work of the Rhine Commission in 1995.

In addition to the ICPRP there are other international initiatives for prevention against flooding. These include the Action Plan on Flood Defence, adopted by all the Rhine states and the EU. The aim of this action plan is to protect people and economic interests against flooding, to improve the Rhine ecosystems and to raise public awareness. Under this action plan the rivers in Nordrhein-Westfalen are being widened, flood retention basins created and dikes strengthened. Also on the cards is an Interreg study of future river discharges, the effectiveness of flood prevention measures and disaster management by Nordrhein-Westfalen, the Dutch authorities and the province of Gelderland. To reduce safety risks, eleven areas in Germany have been designated as overflow areas for the Rhine. Four of these areas are retention basins, with a total capacity of 75 million cubic metres; in the other areas the river bed will be widened by moving the dikes back. These measures will reduce the height of the river during peak discharges by 10 cm (Gordijn et al 2003b).

The Meuse and Scheldt river basins

In 1994 the Netherlands, France, the Walloon Region, the Brussels Urban Region and Flanders signed the Treaties for the Protection of the Meuse and Scheldt Rivers. Under these treaties two commissions were established: the International Commission for the Protection of the Meuse (ICPM) and the International Commission for the Protection of the Scheldt (ICPS). The treaties focus primarily on water quality in the main channel of the river. Ecological restoration receives less priority and groundwater and surface water volumes have only been on the agenda for the last few years. The spatial consequences have so far been limited.

Until 2002 there was also talk of an action plan for the Meuse: the Meuse Flood Action Plan between the Netherlands, Belgium, Luxembourg and France. New treaties have now been signed by these countries and further agreements will be finalised over the next few years; what exactly these will cover is not clear yet. In anticipation of these, the province of Limburg, Flanders and the Walloon Region have entered into a cooperation agreement and the Walloon Region has undertaken to retain water in stream valleys and minor tributaries, create retention basins and overflow areas, deepen the river channel and strengthen the river banks.

The Eems-Dollard river basin

In 1996 a protocol for water and habitat management was added to the existing treaty, which is limited to navigation issues. A sub-commission under the Permanent German-Dutch Transboundary Water Commission (PGC) has been established to oversee this protocol. Its tasks are less detailed than the corresponding ones for the Meuse, Scheldt and Rhine.

land uses, the creation of buffer areas and water retention areas, and habitat restoration and creation) they have considerable and demonstrable spatial consequences.

Water quality policies
EU policies on water quality consist of a number of legislative instruments: the Bathing Water Quality Directive (76/160/EEC), the Nitrates Directive (91/676/EEC) and the Water Framework Directive (2000/60/EC). These will be discussed in turn.

The Bathing Water Quality Directive aims to improve the quality of coastal (sea water) and inland (freshwater) bathing waters. This is enforced by two instruments: water quality standards (which are gradually being tightened) and especially by the 'name, fame and shame' method because a good name is all-important in the recreation industry. These regulations allow the public to find out where it is safe to swim. In the Netherlands there are 634 registered bathing waters; 557 are freshwater facilities and 98 per cent of these meet the required quality standards. This directive has drawn a lot of criticism: the data are often out of date and data from different Member States are difficult to compare. Moreover, the registered (and monitored) bathing waters are not widely publicised in the Netherlands; at most, the public only has access to current information on levels of blue-green algae, for example, via teletext. This directive will therefore have little spatial impact in the Netherlands. It is being revised to bring it up to date, both from a scientific and administrative point of view, and the European Commission put a new draft directive before the European Parliament in October 2002.

The Nitrates Directive (91/676/EEC) is much more important from both an environmental and economic point of view as it sets limits on the nitrate concentrations in groundwater and surface waters. It will also have implications for spatial developments. In the Netherlands this has led to serious problems with implementation because the standards set have proved to be difficult to achieve owing to the extremely high numbers of pigs and chickens per square kilometre (densities rarely found in any other country). The resulting nitrate surpluses cause the greatest problems in the areas of sandy soils in the East and South of the country, where nitrates leach from manure produced by the intensive livestock holdings and pollute the groundwater. Dutch manure legislation is the result of a complicated set of compromises, and as a consequence, emissions are often too high. In 1998 the European Commission summoned the Netherlands to appear before the European Court of Justice and on 2 October 2003 the Court decided in favour of the European Commission on most points. The Dutch official nutrient declaration system (Minas: the Minerals Accounting System) was found to be inadequate for achieving the standards set by the Nitrate Directive and the Netherlands will have to introduce a set of application standards (instead of the current loss standards) for the maximum amount of manure per hectare. This decision will lead to new consultations with the Commission on its implementation and on obtaining an agreement on specific derogations. While Denmark, for example, tries to find a solution by limiting the number of animals per hectare, the Netherlands traditionally takes a more technological approach (feed, nutrient management/accounting, special livestock sheds). This makes it impossible at the moment to predict the scale of the consequences of this decision for the intensive livestock sector in the Netherlands. Besides, the Commission is currently taking similar infringement proceedings for inadequate implementation of this directive against all the other Member States, except Sweden and Denmark.

Water Framework Directive (WFD)
The Water Framework Directive (2000/60/EC) introduces a new system of integrated water policy, under which all waters (including groundwater) will eventually be subject to a coordinated set of water quality standards. The working of this directive is rather insidious: initially it just requires Member States to identify and classify water bodies and flows, but gradually this will develop into a comprehensive monitoring system with stringent standards which cannot easily be avoided and which could have far-reaching consequences for land use in the Netherlands. Indeed, compliance with these standards could prove so problematic that the Dutch may have little alternative than to ask the European Commission for clemency.

The WFD has a long history. Member States of the European Union are signatories to the UN Convention on the Protection and Use of Transboundary Watercourses and International Lakes (the Helsinki Convention of 1992). This convention takes a catchment area approach to water policy, in which the participating countries undertake to apply more stringent measures for the protection and ecologically responsible use of transboundary surface waters and groundwater. They are also committed to taking source-directed measures to reduce and prevent water pollution. The basic principles underlying the convention are the precautionary principle, the polluter pays principle, and the principle that water management problems should not be shifted to other environmental compartments or onto future generations. The convention seeks to establish appropriate environmental measures, best practices and sustainable water resources management, including the application of the ecosystems approach.

The European Union has picked up on the Helsinki Convention to revise the existing water directives and incorporate them into an integrated approach for each catchment area. In 2000 this led to the adoption of the Water Framework Directive (WFD) for the protection of surface water, transitional waters, coastal waters and groundwater. The aim of the Directive is to prevent further deterioration and protect and enhance the status of aquatic ecosystems and, with regard to their water needs, terrestrial ecosystems and wetlands directly depending on the aquatic ecosystems. A further aim is to ensure the progressive reduction of pollution of groundwater and prevent its further pollution, and to contribute to mitigating the effects of floods and droughts. There are few concrete criteria for this last objective, however, and little or no practical progress has been made so far.

As the name implies, the WFD is a framework directive: it places other directives and international agreements within a framework and, in effect, harmonises them. The main international agreement is the Helsinki Water Convention of 1992. In time, other agreements will expire, such as the Directive on the quality required of surface water intended for the abstraction of drinking water in the Member States (1975/440/EEC) and the Decision establishing a common procedure for the exchange of information on the quality of surface fresh water in the Community (1977/795/EEC). In addition to the above-mentioned environmental objectives, the WFD calls for the sustainable use of water. This requires a careful consideration of different interests and raising awareness among the public (household use) and in the agricultural and industrial sectors of the consequences of their actions for water quality; it calls for an economic analysis that clearly reveals what these consequences are. In short, the WFD is based on the premise that water is not a standard commodity, but a birthright that has to be protected.

Time schedule of the WFD
The first hurdle to be taken is to describe the current quality of groundwater and surface waters and the objectives to be achieved. This information must be delivered to the European Commission in December 2004. Two years later (2006), a monitoring plan must be operational and three years after that there must be a detailed plan to implement the objectives and a final adopted river basin management plan (both in 2009). These are to be followed by a plan for the implementation of water services (2010) and a number of consultation rounds to evaluate and assess the objectives.

Table 10. Time schedule for the European Water Framework Directive

Year	Deadline
2000	WFD adopted by the European Parliament
2003	WFD implemented by each Member State
2004	Description and analysis of water bodies
2006	Monitoring programme operational
2009	River basin management plan adopted (may be revised every six years)
2009	Action plan for achieving WFD quality objectives
2010	Implementation of water services
2012	First evaluation of the WFD by the EU
2015	First deadline for achieving the WFD objectives
2021	Second deadline for achieving the WFD objectives
2027	Last deadline for achieving the WFD objectives

Source: RIZA – National Institute for Inland Water Management and Wastewater Treatment

Elaboration of the WFD
For the purposes of determining the quality objectives and drawing up the management plans the EU has been divided into river basin districts, which are further subdivided into river basins. At the lowest level, these river basins are divided into water bodies. A management plan must be drawn up for each river

basin and quality objectives adopted for each water body. This division into subareas makes it possible to introduce spatial differentiation within water policy (see Figure 18).

River basins
A river basin is a geographical unit, an 'area of land from which all surface run-off flows through a sequence of streams, rivers and, possibly, lakes into the sea at a single river mouth, estuary or delta'. Management plans have to be drawn up for each river basin by the end of 2009 and the objectives must be achieved by 22 December 2015. This date can be put back by two periods of six years; the final deadline for achieving the objectives is 2027. The Netherlands contains parts of four river basins: the Rhine, the Meuse, the Eems and the Scheldt.

Water bodies
Within each river basin the Member States are required to identify the location and boundaries of water bodies; transboundary water bodies should be identified as far as possible by the neighbouring countries concerned. According to the text of the directive, these should be defined as discrete and significant elements of surface water or distinct volumes of groundwater within an aquifer or aquifers. The degree to which river basins are divided up into water bodies depends on the balance between the obligation to provide an adequate description of the status of the water bodies and the need to avoid identifying an unmanageable number of them. The North Sea coast should also be considered when designating water bodies; the WFD is valid up to one nautical mile from the coast for ecology and to 12 nautical miles for priority and black list substances. This means that the WFD offers little protection for the ecology of the North Sea because fishing occurs mainly outside the protection zone. The WFD also sets objectives for areas already protected by Community legislation, such as water bodies used for the abstraction of drinking water, bathing waters, ecologically protected areas and areas described in the Habitats and Birds Directives (further explained in Chapter 'Environment and Nature'). The boundaries of the water bodies shown in Figure 18, for example, have not yet all been determined and adopted and working groups are currently studying about 1000 water bodies.

Surface waters may be divided into three main categories: natural waters, heavily modified water bodies and artificial water bodies. These include not only the water itself, but also the shores, banks and the terrestrial ecosystems directly depending on the water bodies. Water in the first category – natural waters – can be divided into rivers, lakes, transitional waters and coastal waters, which can be identified according to a number of morphological, geological, chemical and hydrological characteristics. Elbertsen et al (2003) have drawn up a proposed typology for the Netherlands. Differentiating between natural and heavily modified water bodies is much more difficult. The definition of the latter is 'a body of surface water which as a result of physical alterations by human activity is substantially changed in character'. An artificial water body is 'a body of surface water created by human activity', such as the Nieuwe Merwede and the Nieuwe Waterweg. How artificial water bodies can be

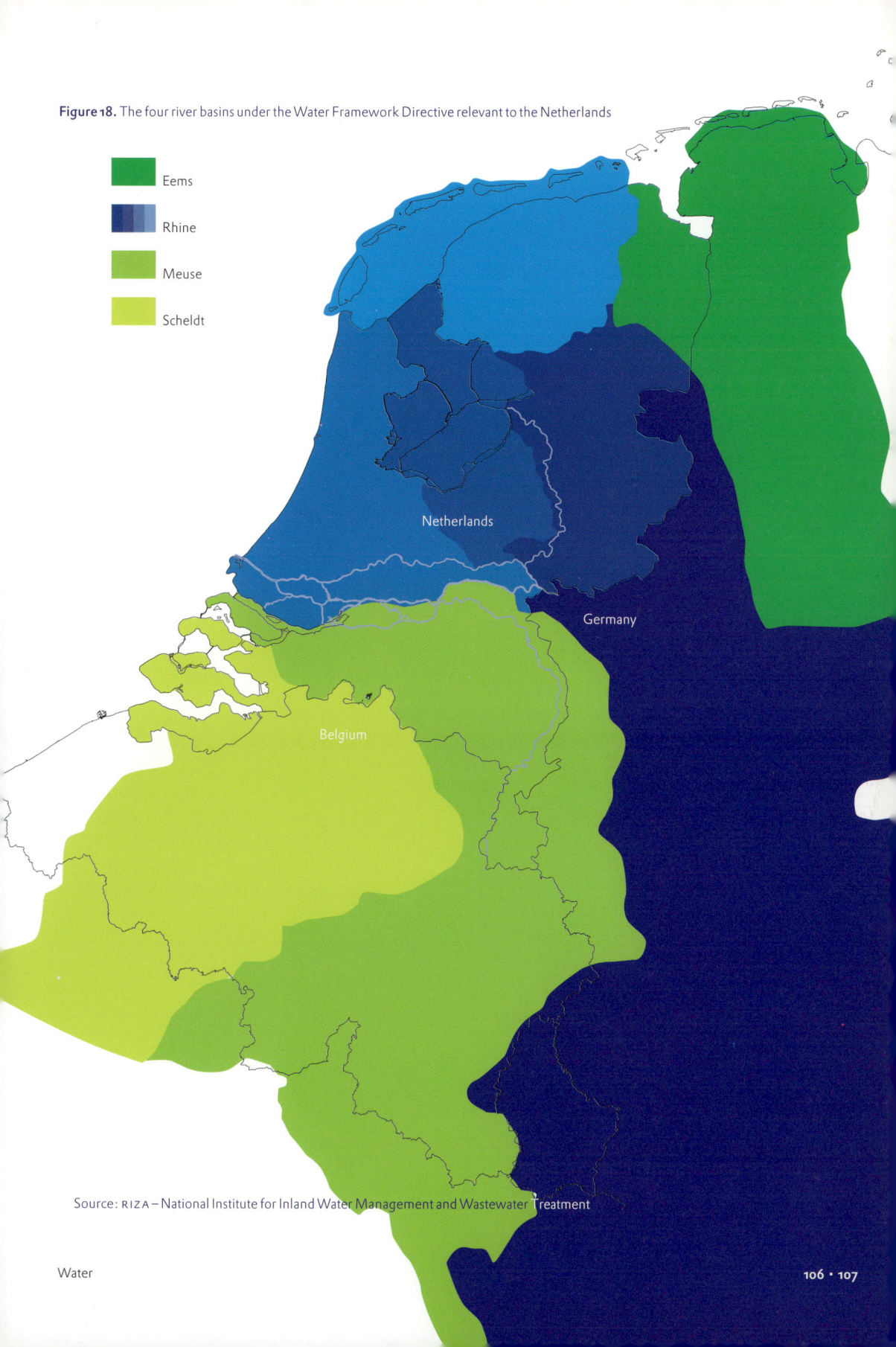

Figure 18. The four river basins under the Water Framework Directive relevant to the Netherlands

- Eems
- Rhine
- Meuse
- Scheldt

Source: RIZA – National Institute for Inland Water Management and Wastewater Treatment

Water

Water is an international issue

In the Netherlands the river basins of the four main rivers are the river basins as laid down in the WFD. These rivers flow through many countries, all of which may take a different approach to their management. As the Netherlands lies downstream of all the other countries it has little chance of achieving the objectives for the Dutch water bodies.

The Dutch North Sea coast counts as a separate water body (or may be divided into several water bodies). But because it forms a part of the four Dutch river basins this presents a problem: some of the pollution comes from the South, beyond the Dutch border. This pollution in turn influences the North Sea coast to the North. So, as far as the North Sea is concerned, the Netherlands also has to deal with countries outside these river basins, such as France and England, but also Denmark and Sweden. International agreements on water will have to be reached, despite the fact that none of these other countries shares a river basin with the Netherlands. This can complicate the whole process of setting quality standards for the North Sea and achieving these standards.

The Interreg subsidies already have an impact on the Dutch border regions. These areas have always suffered the greatest problems because solving them has always been put on the back burner through a lack of urgency and too little appreciation of the needs on both sides of the border. With Interreg subsidies now available for tackling these problems, border regions are going to be the test beds for innovative concepts in water management, the impacts of which will be felt in these regions themselves. These regions will be strengthened by the WFD: the FWD takes a river basin approach, and because river basins do not respect national borders, integrated plans will emerge that will explicitly recognise border regions.

Nitrogen

Nitrogen is one of the most important nutrients for living organisms. In a natural freshwater environment, the main sources of available nitrogen are mineralisation and fixation processes. The nitrogen compounds thus formed enrich the soil or leach into surface waters. This means that the lower reaches of a river are naturally relatively rich in nitrogen. Under anaerobic conditions in the groundwater and streambeds, nitrate is broken down again by bacteria to form nitrogen gas or the greenhouse gas nitrous oxide (N_2O), depending on the efficiency of conversion. Human activities tend to raise nitrogen concentrations to levels far higher than the natural background: fertilisation of agricultural land has led to nitrogen concentrations in rivers and streams ten times higher than the natural background concentrations; discharges from sewage works raise levels even further.

When nitrogen concentrations reach very high levels, there is a high risk of an explosion in the growth of microorganisms, making it impossible for all but a limited number of other species to survive: this process is called eutrophication. The other nutrient commonly responsible for eutrophication is phosphorus (see text box on phosphorus). In some cases, the addition of nitrogen to the environment can lead to life-threatening conditions. To achieve the WFD standards existing policy instruments may have to be worked up in more detail or new policy instruments developed. It may be interesting to see which instruments are developed or used in other countries, and if they could be applied successfully in the Netherlands.

Phosphorus

Like nitrogen, phosphorus is an important nutrient for living organisms. In natural situations the soil contains low levels of phosphate because the conversion of minerals to ions is a slow process. Fertilisation has raised the background concentrations of phosphate to fifteen times the natural levels, in most parts of the Netherlands by leaching from agricultural land. Phosphorus easily binds to soil particles in soils and in the beds of rivers and streams. Excessive concentrations of phosphorus causes eutrophication in lakes and ponds, which can lead to algal blooms and the growth of blue-green algae.

Figure 19. Relationship between phosphorus levels and the P standard in 2015, moderate scenario

Figure 20. Relationship between nitrate levels and the N standard in 2015, moderate scenario

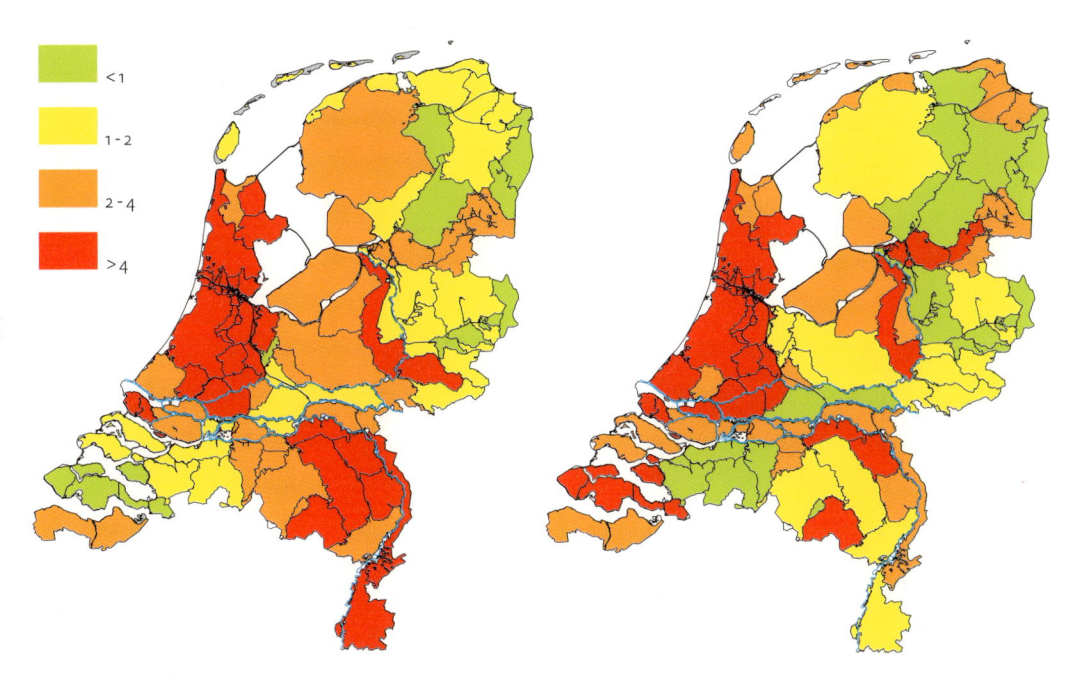

- < 1
- 1 - 2
- 2 - 4
- > 4

Source: Van der Bolt et al. (2003)

subdivided into water bodies is not yet clear. It is possible that the 'polder water level areas' (*polderpeilgebieden*) will be chosen and, where canals are involved, the areas between important locks.

Two proposals have been made for dividing groundwater into water bodies. Both Meinardi (2003) and the Technical Commission on Soil Protection (TCB 2001) use the geological characteristics of the subsoil and the hydrology of the area, but identify totally different areas. That similar approaches can lead to considerably different outcomes can be explained by the fact that Meinardi has drawn up a new classification, while the TCB based their study on a much earlier inventory of groundwater systems. Clearly, a standard system for the Netherlands is urgently needed.

Quality objectives
The six categories of surface water are further subdivided into types, based on the physical and chemical factors that determine the characteristics of each category, and therefore its ecological status. The EU objective for natural waters is 'good ecological status' and for artificial and heavily modified water bodies is a 'good ecological potential', which is less ambitious. For groundwater these objectives are defined as a 'good quantitative status', which refers to a healthy balance between abstraction and the natural recharge of groundwater by precipitation, and a 'good chemical status', which refers to substances

not naturally occurring in (local) groundwater and which are dangerous to humans and the ecological status.

Consequences for the Netherlands

Water has always been a critical issue in the Netherlands. The coastline makes up half its borders, it is situated in the deltas of three rivers and two-thirds of the country lies beneath sea level. For hundreds of years the country has known an extensive water management system, with its own administrative bodies, the *waterschappen,* or water boards. Water management now treats the quantitative and qualitative aspects in relation to each other under an 'integrated water policy'.

The consequences of EU water policy for the Netherlands primarily relate to achieving the standards set by the Nitrates Directive and the Water Framework Directive, and so these will receive much attention here. We should bear in mind that meeting these standards must be coupled with other objectives, such as flood prevention and safety measures.

The challenge of meeting quality standards

As we have seen in the sections on the Nitrates Directive and the Water Framework Directive, groundwater and surface waters must meet certain minimum quality standards. The WFD standards still have to be fixed, but we can expect that these will be strictly enforced once they are; this was found to be the case for the Nitrates Directives. We can even expect that the nitrate standards under the WFD will be tighter than the current national standards and those set by the Nitrates Directive. The 50 mg N/l for groundwater has little ecological relevance: it is a drinking water standard. An ecological standard would be more like 25 mg N/l or lower.

At the moment the national Maximum Permissible Risk (MPR) level is far from being met in both surface water and groundwater: not for pesticides; not for heavy metals; and not for nitrogen and phosphorus. This has been found in studies by the Commissie Integraal Waterbeheer (2002), from analyses by water boards and studies by the National Institute for Public Health and the Environment (RIVM) (Willems et al. 2002; Meinardi et al. 2003). Neither is current policy able to bring us any closer to the objectives, so we know already that the Netherlands faces a considerable challenge.

An initial exploratory study by Alterra (van der Bolt et al. 2003) on this issue revealed that relatively little effort is needed to reduce pollution by pesticides: if the source of pollution is close to a water body and high standards are maintained, only a few pesticides will be present at concentrations slightly above permissible levels (see Figures 19 and 20). However, the situation for fertilisers is quite different, and in this respect the WFD poses a significant threat to current agricultural practices in the Netherlands. Nitrate itself is not actually the biggest problem. Under anaerobic conditions some of the nitrogen is released to the atmosphere as N_2 gas (see text box on nitrogen). Phosphorus, on the other hand, presents a much greater problem and will have to be actively removed from the soil and water system (see text box on phosphorus). In many areas the soil already contains so much phosphorus (particularly in peat and clay soils) that the soil will have to be cleaned up to prevent a continuous leaching of phosphorus to surface waters, even when no more fertiliser is applied. There is only one way to do this: remove the soil.

If ambitions are set at even a moderate level (achieving a good ecological status) drastic measures will still have to be taken: just one-third of the current surface area devoted to agriculture can remain in production. In the areas of clay and peaty soils in Noord-Holland and Zuid-Holland and the sandy soils of Noord-Brabant, the reduction goals will never be achieved because of replenishment from reserves in the soil and groundwater seepage. Simply taking these areas out of agricultural production is insufficient. If the WFD standards are higher than the current MPR values, drastic changes will have to be made to current agricultural practices, particularly in the west of the country.

If ambitions are high (very good ecological status) the entire country will become unsuitable for agriculture. But that is not all: this objective will be impossible to achieve throughout virtually the whole country because of replenishment from the soil, which will have to be removed. This is an unrealistic option. Whatever the case, farming practices will have to change, if only because the European Court of Justice, in response to the breach of the Nitrate Directive, has ordered the Netherlands to pursue a different fertiliser policy. This will make agriculture less competitive and may drive it from all but the most fertile soils with the fewest water problems.

In any case, the Netherlands has signed up to the WFD, which means that the causes of the pollution of surface waters and groundwater will have to be tackled. The blame for the excessive levels of nutrients can be put at the door of the intensive land-based farming sector. Pollution by pesticides can also be largely attributed to agriculture, but the maintenance of streets (weed control) is a major contributing factor as well (Lijzen and Ekelenkamp 1995). A significant source of groundwater pollution can be traced to leakage from a range of urban sources (sewers, car maintenance, gardens, etc.) while atmospheric deposits contribute, to a lesser extent, to background levels in groundwater and surface waters (Pieterse et al. 2002).

There are many ways to tackle the sources of pollution. The Alterra study (van der Bolt et al. 2003) revealed that taking agricultural land out of production will have the greatest effect. In new urban areas the solution is to build at lower densities. Unfortunately, the excessive nitrate concentrations in groundwater and surface waters and the excessive phosphate concentrations in surface waters is a result of overfertilisation in the past. If tackling the problem at the source will not help, effect-oriented measures can be taken, one option being to restructure water systems and create buffer zones and reed beds; such measures would have a considerable spatial impact. Besides taking agricultural land out of production, this impact has not been quantified in the Alterra study. For heavy metals, alternative techniques may have a significant effect (e.g. not using zinc gutters, etc.), but such techniques are extremely expensive.

Another problem in the discussion on achieving the EU standards is the cultural difference between the European Commission and the Netherlands (see final chapter). In the Netherlands it does not really matter if the water management authorities do not achieve the agreed standards, they just have to make a convincing case that they have made every effort to do so. This obligation to make every effort to achieve compliance stands in sharp contrast to the obligation to achieve a result expected by the EU. If the standards have not been achieved in 2007 (the final deadline), the Netherlands will be fined. This fine will be substantial – and more may follow. As a result, the Netherlands will need to take far-reaching (spatial) measures. In view of this, it would be sensible to take action soon to allow time to assess the effects.

Impact on spatial planning
The obligatory nature of the Nitrates Directive and the WFD will give the water sector greater weight within spatial and land use planning policy, at least as far as the achievement of the objectives require spatial measures. It is simply no longer possible to ignore the fact that certain water quality standards have to be achieved and that some developments are just not acceptable. It is too early to estimate how this will affect policy, but there is a chance that in some regions water management will provide the underlying policy framework and set conditions that other sectors will have to meet. The water management authorities in the provinces of Noord-Holland, Zuid-Holland and Noord-Brabant will certainly have their work cut out for them.

The existing statutory instruments are considered inadequate for achieving the water management objectives. New instruments are now being developed, such as the urban and municipal water plan, the 'water opportunity map' (*waterkansenkaart*), the 'subcatchment area management plan' (*deelstroomgebiedbeheerplan*), the 'water assessment' (*watertoets*) in land use plans, and the 'catchment area management plan' (*stroomgebiedbeheersplan*) (Bosma and van Dijk 2003). Many of these instruments, however, have been developed to prevent flooding and have little to do with European regulations. It seems logical that these instruments will be expanded to include international components.

Although spatial measures have a clear role to play in flood prevention, it is unlikely that the European Commission will oblige or urge Member States to introduce spatial measures in this area. At the moment, Dutch authorities have a tendency to allow a little bit of everything: a little bit of housing, employment, water and natural habitat. The European regulations (including the Habitats and Birds Directives; see Chapter 'Environment and nature') will possibly cause a shift in thinking towards a more sectoral approach: not a bit of everything, but primarily a certain type of land use. In areas vulnerable to surface water pollution, for example, water and natural habitats will take precedence. Tightening up the rules is unlikely to be sufficient for achieving the standards set down in the WFD; physical space will have to be freed up, both for reducing the discharge of hazardous substances (such as establishing buffer zones, reducing the area of agricultural land and laying out reed beds and other marshland areas for water purification) and for restoring river and stream systems (such as reintroducing meanders and natural banks). In addition, opportunities will be available to bring in measures to improve water quality on the back of flood prevention measures. In the west of the Netherlands the risk of flooding is such that the creation of retention basins may be necessary, and it may be possible to design these in such a way that they help to achieve water quality objectives.

Impact on administrative boundaries
As stated above, the number of designated WFD water bodies must be manageable, while at the same time sufficient for achieving the objectives as well as possible. The same standards should be achievable within these boundaries, making it conceivable that different policies will have to apply to different water bodies within the same administrative area, such as the area controlled by a water board or province. This may make it necessary to redraw some administrative boundaries, for example by subdividing or merging water boards. In addition, the chosen scale determines how the water authority can work with local stakeholders, administrators and residents. In the Netherlands, with its many polders, the bigger the water body the more difficult the process will be.

It is expected that the delineation of the water bodies will largely follow the boundaries of the existing subcatchment areas as adopted in the area-based policy and the 'water management for the 21st century' policy in order to avoid creating yet another administrative tier. Despite this, there is a considerable danger that policy for the management of water bodies will conflict with integrated area-based policies; in particular because solutions for achieving water quality objectives are not always good solutions for other water management objectives, such as the storage and retention of water.

Conclusions

Water is fundamental to the spatial structure of the Netherlands, and the ramifications of EU water policy in the long term can be considerable. Given this, it is still safe to say that there are relatively few discernable direct impacts of EU water policy on spatial developments so far. Part of this, of course, is because the full spatial impact of the KRW will only become apparent in the future once measures are taken to comply with its provisions. EU water policy is therefore a prime example of the indirect spatial workings of EU sectoral policy: its direct manifestations remain unseen, while its indirect effects reverberate in the kinds of alliances forged at the international level and the measures taken domestically to comply with EU regulations.

Already the Netherlands is working closely with other countries to resolve the problems of safety, flooding and water quality, and this cooperation will probably intensify. The Netherlands will sign more bilateral and multilateral agreements in the future, partly for the implementation and elaboration of European directives, but also to tackle local problems. This last trend is already observable in the Interreg studies. In the interests of public safety, retention areas are being established in Germany and the dikes near the border are being raised. Some areas are being restructured to cope with high water and prevent flooding by creating wetter areas and restoring meanders to allow a more natural water system to develop. Under the banner of water quality and nature conservation, standards are being raised and sewer systems upgraded.

It is to be expected that the WFD standards will be more stringent than the Dutch MPR values and that meeting these standards will present a considerable challenge. Solutions can entail significant spatial interventions, such as the creation of buffer zones, reduction of agricultural production and the placement of reed beds. The fact that meeting the MPR standards has proved difficult enough means that even greater efforts will be required in future. It is quite conceivable that the Netherlands will ask the EU for an exemption from the requirements, for less stringent standards or for a postponement of the deadline for achieving the standards.

Further research

We do not know how much space will be needed to achieve the WFD standards. How many buffer zones will be needed? How much farmland should be pulled out of production; how many streams and rivers will have to be restored to a more natural, meandering course? Alterra has conducted a quick-scan study of the effects of the WFD, which was based on many assumptions and covered a large scale. A further study will be needed to investigate the influence on land uses other than agriculture, specifically taking into account the spatial consequences for measures like the creation of buffer zones. The follow-up study should also consider groundwater because achieving good quality groundwater may require setting certain standards for (new) urban areas. In addition, attention should also be paid to saltwater bodies (the Wadden Sea and the North Sea), about which there has been little or no discussion.

Spatial Policy Issues and the EU

SPATIAL POLICY ISSUES AND THE EU

The purpose of this chapter is to consider three major and topical policy issues in Dutch spatial planning and expose the – usually unseen – influence of EU policy. For each topic we present a table summarising the issues and provide, where possible, an estimate of future EU involvement. Much of the information is drawn from earlier chapters. The three selected policy areas are urban development strategy, mainport policy and rural development. Space and time constraints have prevented the inclusion of many other topics that also illustrate the EU's influence. Perhaps others will explore these in future studies.

Urban development policy

Nowhere in Europe is the pressure on the countryside greater than in the Netherlands. Not only is it the most densely populated Member State, it also has the highest density of roads, waterways, railways and power lines, and the most intensive horticulture and livestock farming sectors. Foreigners often marvel at how every square metre of the country seems to have been put to some productive use; but this has come at a price: not only are some functions difficult to reconcile (e.g. airports and residential development) but intensive land use can also lead to an unacceptably high concentration of environmental problems (e.g. water pollution from intensive livestock farming and air pollution in and around urban areas). It is not surprising, therefore, that spatial planning policy continues to occupy a relatively high position on the Dutch political agenda.

Planning is not new to the Netherlands. Indeed, nowhere else in Europe is the imprint of human activity more evident: the very shape and form of the country is the product of centuries of massive land reclamation and intensive water management. After the Second World War the question of where and how to build became a matter of national priority. During the past forty years, four policy documents on spatial planning have been produced to provide a strategic vision for urban development in the country. Over the years, these documents have set out a number of widely acclaimed policies, such as the growth centres and clustered deconcentration, and some less applauded ones, such as the ABC location policy (Faludi and van der Valk 1994; van der Cammen and De Klerk 2003). In the 1990s work began on a Fifth National Policy Document on Spatial Planning, but in May 2002, after many years of research and public debate, the government fell and the document was shelved just weeks before the final version was due to be ratified. This means that the national policy on urban development contained in the Fourth National Policy Document (the 'Vinex') still remains in force. Published in 1991, this policy predates the establishment of the European Union (Maastricht Treaty). At present, the Ministry of Spatial Planning, Housing and the Environment

(VROM) is busy preparing a new national policy document to replace the Vinex policy. But how has the additional factor of the EU changed the capacity for and nature of spatial planning in the Netherlands? And how will this be addressed in any subsequent policy document?

Current urban development policy
Dutch urban development policy is going through a period of transition. The statutory planning document remains the Vinex, but a statement of intent issued in Autumn 2002 by the then planning minister charted a new course for urban development policy which deviates in some fundamental ways from both the Vinex and the now defunct Fifth National Policy Document. Drawing on these two documents, we will make a few observations about the national spatial planning policy now in force, and how this corresponds or conflicts with various EU sectoral policies.

The left-of-centre administration that came to power in November 1989 made the amelioration of environmental damage caused by a sharp increase in mobility one of the main goals of spatial planning. To this end, one of the principal policies in the Vinex was the promotion of new housing development on brownfield land (in urban areas) or in greenfield urban extensions (the 'Vinex locations'). This policy was supplemented by a location policy for businesses that classified enterprises into A, B, or C categories on the basis of their activities and number of visitors, and designated appropriate locations for them (i.e. businesses with many employees or visitors should be concentrated near public transportation facilities and locations along the motorway were reserved for production and distribution companies). Retail outlets have been subjected to an even stricter regime, with an all-out ban on out-of-town shopping malls since the 1970s (Evers 2002). In addition to this heavily prescriptive regulation of locations for new homes and businesses, the Vinex also contained policies to delineate and protect the Green Heart (the relatively open area between the four major cities of the Randstad urban agglomeration in the west of the country). Locations for new residential, commercial and recreational areas were subject to five general criteria:
– proximity to the city centre
– connection to public transportation
– a balance between residential, work, recreation and green spaces
– keeping the open countryside free of urbanisation to preserve its ecological and agricultural value
– feasibility of implementation.

In short, the Vinex policies focused on concentrating urban functions and retaining open space. A consequence is the promotion of high-density development. Now, more than a decade later, it is relevant to ask how this policy stance fares in the current European Union context. Although this position would in essence be lauded by the EU as contributing to what it considers to be sustainable development, its continuation could bring the Netherlands into conflict with some other policy areas.

First of all, it should be noted that conducting a restrictive policy to protect open landscapes will become more difficult because of the far-reaching reform of the EU's agricultural policy. The spatial planning policy that put rural areas out-of-bounds for urban development was made possible, in part, by production subsidies that encouraged Dutch farmers to continue to work the land. Paying farmers to let land lie fallow (set-aside) is much more difficult to justify when demand for new housing is high. This, of course, is equally applicable to low-density and high-density development.

Concentrating future building in already densely populated areas can exacerbate certain environmental problems; and if this means that certain EU standards are exceeded, further development could be jeopardised. Air quality is the most obvious example. Since the Netherlands is already approaching the maximum levels of air pollution (NO_2 and particulates) for 2010, this could, in theory, preclude all major traffic-generating developments after this date. Even now, policies generally prohibit the building of facilities such as hospitals and day-care centres in areas with poor air quality, which limits opportunities for urban infill: air quality standards nearly frustrated plans for a football stadium in The Hague; Maastricht cannot approve any future building plans at all without exceeding EU guidelines on fine particulates; and some bus routes in Amsterdam city centre have been modified to improve the air quality in certain streets. Similarly, current plans to build on top of motorways may founder – apart from the difficulty of financing such expensive projects – simply because the air pollution exceeds EU standards. Although no policy has yet been drafted on electromagnetic radiation levels (this is still being studied by the EU), possible standards for minimum distances between homes and power lines and mobile phone masts could also limit the prospects for infill development.

EU water policy can affect the prospects for urban development as well, although this applies to both high-density and low-density development. Since the entire Netherlands falls under one of four designated river basin districts, plans for urban growth may come into conflict with objectives of the Water Framework Directive, such as reducing pollution, preserving protected areas and restoring and enhancing bodies of surface water. The designation of safe swimming water according to EU criteria can affect the market for housing near rivers and lakes.

Other actions which can fall foul of EU legislation are the methods used to achieve further urban concentration. Government authorities frequently encourage businesses to locate in central areas by offering tax incentives or making land available at below market value. The EU now considers this to be a form of state aid, which is subject to restrictions. Moreover, regeneration schemes which involve some kind of a public-private partnership or substantial public investment may be subject to EU policies on competitive tendering.

On the other hand, the goal of concentration may be facilitated somewhat by regional cohesion policy: since the last Structural Funds period, cities may vie for Objective 2 funding, and the Urban programme has been in existence for the past two periods. Making cities more attractive places to live may ease the demand for suburban or rural housing, and in the future such efforts could be enhanced by experience with best practices generated by the Urban and Interreg programmes and data supplied by ESPON. Moreover, any aid for rural areas (either in the form of income support for farmers or for converting agricultural land into nature reserves) will help to curb the urge to sell rural land for new housing. Whether or not this outweighs the disadvantages Dutch farmers experience as a result of the reform of the agricultural policy remains to be seen. We will return to this vitally important issue in the next section.

Anticipated urban development policy
A little over a decade after the publication of the environmentally-oriented Vinex, and a few months after the fiasco surrounding the Fifth National Policy Document, the newly elected right-of-centre government (2002) emerged with a letter of intent (*stellingnamebrief*) that preached virtually the opposite of current planning policy. The guiding principle was to grant more latitude to the workings of the free market, cut red tape and accommodate residential preferences. A recent study by the Netherlands Institute for Spatial Research has revealed a considerable demand for 'rural' environments near cities (van Dam et al. 2003). The prospect of a relaxation of the restrictive policy on development in the open countryside could pave the way for more diffuse patterns of urban growth, which would run up against other European Union policies and regulations.

The European ecological network, Natura 2000, poses the most formidable impediment to urban development. As a majority of natural habitats are outside urban areas, the protected areas policy will have a greater impact on the prospects for diffuse urban development. As explained in the Chapter 'Environment and Nature', if a particular area is designated a natural habitat, permitting development is no longer a matter of national discretion, but has to be referred to the European Commission. A very good case has to be made; a mere desire for more homes in a natural environment is not sufficient. This fact is not yet fully appreciated in the Netherlands. Only recently, for example, an urban designer made the headlines with an iconoclastic plan to build villas in natural areas, but such a plan has little chance of success if the area is protected under EU legislation, regardless of national policy. Similarly, the Water Framework Directive can limit the scale of urban development in areas where it may contribute to an erosion of water quality, and in designated water retention areas that are inundated each year.

We should add that although diffuse urban development may not directly conflict with certain sectors of EU policy, it does run counter to the spirit and principles of various European policy areas. For example, low-density detached housing development (urban sprawl) is considered to be energy inefficient and harmful to the environment because it encourages car use, and is therefore out of step with the principle of sustainable development; EU transport policy tends to favour rail, which is more amenable to concentrated rather than diffuse development, and the high-speed train will enhance the economic attraction of the areas where it stops; and encouraging urban diffusion (usually manifested as a form of selective suburban migration) can be seen as undermining EU investments in projects under the Urban and Objective 2 (Cities) programmes.

Table 11. Effect of EU policies on urban development in the Netherlands

EU policy	Urban concentration	Urban diffusion
Regional	Urban II, Objective 2 (Cities) and Objective 3 to aid restructuring and social/urban problems	In general, diffusion runs counter to the EU sustainable development ideal
Transport	Support for PBKAL provides an impetus for cities with high-speed train stations	Need for more roads out of step with EU model split policy
Agriculture	Reduction of subsidies may encourage urbanisation of agricultural areas	Reduction of subsidies may encourage urbanisation of agricultural areas
Competition	Limitation of urban renewal policy via caps on state aid	n/a
	Restriction on PPP due to EU tendering regulations	
	Restrictive policy and second home regulations may come under scrutiny	
Environmental	Air pollution standards and possible future regulations on noise or electromagnetic fields may limit infill options	Natura 2000 will make it extremely difficult to allow development in designated habitats
Water	Water quality standards	Water retention areas (annually inundated)

From Table 11 it is clear that both urban diffusion and urban concentration policies encounter different aspects of EU policy. In some cases, rather strict rules apply, and their violation can result in fines or (perhaps even more costly) negative judgements when challenged in court. Other interfaces between EU sectoral policy and Dutch urban development policy are less antagonistic, but nonetheless show a divergence in principles.

Rural areas policy

The Dutch countryside is under considerable pressure and the role of agriculture as the economic driver in rural areas is declining. Already over 90 per cent of the working population in rural areas work outside the agricultural sector – and the end is not yet in sight as the rate of farm closures runs at two to three per cent each year. The demand for land in the countryside for new residential and commercial development is growing, and the claims for nature conservation and water management are greater still (Boekema and van Brussel 2003: 74; Ministerie van VROM 2001b: 128, Part 1). In some areas the intensive use of agricultural land (horticulture, intensive livestock farming) causes serious environmental problems, such as failure to comply with the requirements of the Nitrates Directive (see Chapter 8). Fragmentation of agricultural holdings and unsightly punctuations in the landscape, particularly in the urban fringes and around villages ('horsification'), are further manifestations of this trend. The intense pressure for urban expansion puts the Dutch countryside in an entirely different position to rural areas in Southern Europe (e.g. in France, Spain and Greece), where the economic position of rural areas is weakening and the thinly populated and often hilly or mountainous areas tend to suffer from erosion and depopulation and where there is open talk of rural dereliction, and even total abandonment of the land.

Rural development is not a new area of policy; it was already a part of the European structural policies in 1972 and is closely tied to agricultural policy. It has now become a portmanteau term. It gained official status at the 1996 European Conference on Rural Development and was adopted in the Cork Declaration. To a large extent, it is a policy reaction to the negative impacts of the traditional (production-oriented) European agricultural policy, which have become visible across much of Europe's countryside. Among the aims of rural development stated in the Cork Declaration are 'reversing rural out-migration, combating poverty, stimulating employment and equality of opportunity, and responding to growing requests for more quality, health, safety, personal development and leisure, and improving rural well-being.'[1]

What is Dutch rural areas policy?
In the past the Netherlands has put few spatial restrictions on agriculture, while urban development in the open countryside was contained by imposing building contours, designating green buffer zones and pursuing a restrictive policy on new urban development. The Fourth National Policy Document on Spatial Planning introduced the 'rural areas strategies' (*koersenbeleid*), in which rural regions were marked out for one of four indicative development paths 'which must be taken into account in the land use planning and development of the rural areas' : the green strategy, based on ecological qualities; the yellow strategy, based on intensive agricultural production; the blue strategy, based on regional qualities, with combinations of (extensive) agricultural production, water management, recreation and nature conservation; and the brown strategy, based on land-based agriculture in a 'mosaic' with other land uses, such as forestry, natural habitats and military training grounds. This policy has almost entirely failed through a lack of support and policy tools; it had been dropped by the time the Fifth National Policy Document appeared, which focused on profitable 'landless agriculture' (greenhouse complexes and intensive livestock farming).

Meanwhile, the need to make decisions on the spatial allocation of land uses in rural areas has become even more urgent. In the areas surrounding the cities, where there is a demand for more accessible, park-like recreational areas, agricultural use is becoming even more intensive due to the rising land prices. At the same time, open landscapes are being broken up and occupied by pseudo-agricultural uses (stables and riding schools, hobby farms, warehouses and storage sheds). On the other hand, greenhouse horticulture and intensive livestock farms can benefit considerably from concentration in areas where transport and environmental and energy management can be arranged in the most efficient way (Gordijn et al. 2003).

1. At http://europa.eu.int/comm/agriculture/rur/cork_en.htm

Rural development as a policy term was introduced in the Netherlands in a report by the agriculture ministry called *Dynamiek en Vernieuwing* [Change and Renewal] (Ministerie van LNV 1995), and was explained by the agriculture minister, Laurens Brinkhorst, in a letter to the lower house of the Dutch Parliament under the title *Groene lijnen naar de toekomst* ['Green paths to the future']. This letter lists four aspects of rural development:
- economic competitiveness
- ecological sustainability
- social cohesion
- cultural identity.

In *Vitaal en Samen* [Working Together for a Living Countryside] the Ministry of Agriculture, Nature and Food Quality's policy programme 2004–2007, the agriculture minister, Cees Veerman, continues this policy line, adding a number of specific Government topics, such as cutting the costs of red tape, curbing the proliferation of regulations and strengthening the knowledge economy. These policies clearly build on European policy, in particular Council Regulation (EC) No 1257/1999 of 17 May 1999 on support for rural development (the Rural Development Framework Regulation), which provides the formal basis for the 'second pillar' of the agricultural policy. This in turn forms the basis for the Dutch Rural Development Programme 2000–2006, which contains measures for the whole territory of the Netherlands for the seven-year plan period. The total budget for this programme is 4.8 billion Euros, of which about 1.7 billion Euros will be borne by the European Union (via the Rural Development Framework Regulation, Structural Funds, Interreg IIIB, Leader+, LIFE). The Netherlands has chosen to take a broad approach to rural development in which all the relevant EU subsidies are combined with national and provincial subsidies (Ministerie van LNV 2001). A striking omission in the programme is the lack of a national vision for the spatial interpretation of this policy; the rural development policy measures are generic in nature and apply to the whole of the rural area.

What EU policies affect rural development?
The strong influence exerted by the common agricultural policy on rural development policy has recently been described by Strijker in the proceedings of the Regional Science Association's conference on rural development (Strijker 2003:25–31). Strijker questions whether the Dutch situation satisfies the requirements for receiving EU subsidies for rural development: there is little evidence of real rural poverty, out-migration to the cities or serious quality of life issues arising from a lack of services, as is the case in the southern regions of Europe. He considers European rural development policy to be of little practical use in the Netherlands, unless it is seen as way of obtaining a reasonable share of EU funding. A more positive view is given in *Rural Development, Principles and Practice*, a new textbook by Moseley (2003). This book is based to a large extent on practical examples of projects which have received funding from the Leader programme. Moseley lists five important features of rural development that characterise the Leader approach: area-based, bottom-up, local partnership, and emphasis on innovation and integration (intersectoral).

The great diversity in approaches to rural development in various regions in Europe is well illustrated in the book *Living Countrysides* (van der Ploeg et al. 2002). This contains a report of a socio-economic study of rural development involving more than 3000 farmers in six countries. An interesting result is the opinions of the farmers on the limiting and conducive factors for rural development: 75 per cent mentioned the European Union as an important 'stimulus', while national governments were seen as the 'most important barriers and hindrances' (van der Ploeg et al. 2002: 227). One thing this study makes clear is that the distinctions between traditional, production-oriented agriculture and new forms of multifunctional agriculture are becoming blurred (see Figure 21).

Figure 21. Interrelations between old and new agriculture in the Netherlands

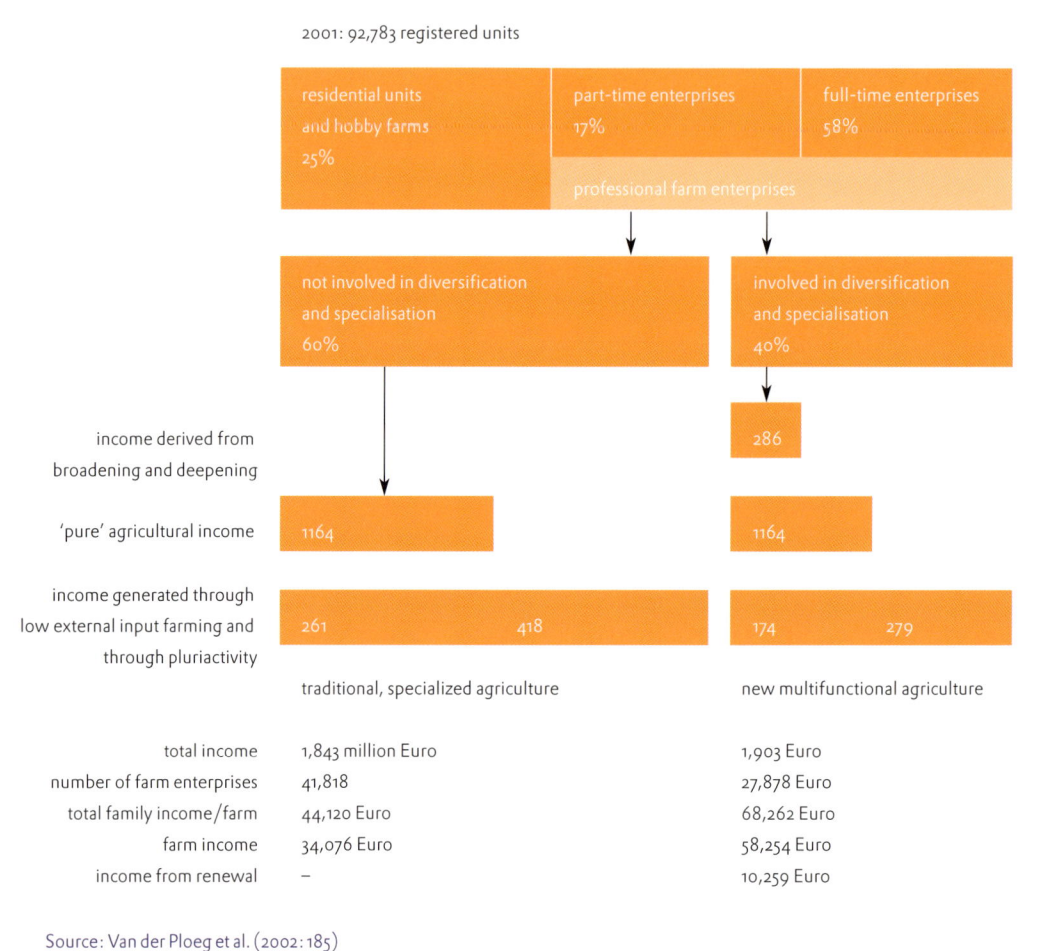

2001: 92,783 registered units

	residential units and hobby farms 25%	part-time enterprises 17%	full-time enterprises 58%
		professional farm enterprises	

	not involved in diversification and specialisation 60%	involved in diversification and specialisation 40%
income derived from broadening and deepening		286
'pure' agricultural income	1164	1164
income generated through low external input farming and through pluriactivity	261 418	174 279
	traditional, specialized agriculture	new multifunctional agriculture
total income	1,843 million Euro	1,903 Euro
number of farm enterprises	41,818	27,878 Euro
total family income/farm	44,120 Euro	68,262 Euro
farm income	34,076 Euro	58,254 Euro
income from renewal	–	10,259 Euro

Source: Van der Ploeg et al. (2002: 185)

Current agricultural policy makes a distinction between 'specialisation' (*verdieping*) and diversification (*verbreding*) of agricultural activities. Specialisation is achieved by increasing net added value per unit of end product compared with traditional farming, for example by developing regional products (e.g. Texels lamb, Beemster cheese), organic farming and developing networks that strengthen the bonds between producers and consumers. Diversification means obtaining additional income from new, not strictly agricultural activities, such as farm campsites, social care farms, energy generation, agri-environmental farming and habitat management, riding stables, etc. The study by van der Ploeg shows that about 40 per cent of 'real' farmers and growers in the Netherlands are involved in diversification or specialisation activities.

In addition to the common agricultural policy and European regional policy, European nature, environmental and water policies also have an important influence on rural areas. The significance of the Nitrates Directive for the intensive livestock farming sector is illustrated by the complicated set of fertiliser and manure regulations introduced in the 1990s to prevent overfertilisation and excessive nitrate concentrations in groundwater and surface waters (see previous chapter). Meanwhile, plans are being drawn up for restructuring the intensive livestock sector in large parts of the country – which is also necessary for veterinary and nature conservation reasons. The significance of the Water Framework Directive for farming in the Netherlands is hard to deny following the publication of the study by Alterra (Van der Bolt et al. 2003), which gives an initial picture of the major consequences for agriculture when the expected new water quality objectives are translated into legal standards. The large-scale intensification of agricultural activities in the Netherlands has had negative impacts on soil quality which can only be reversed by a drastic and long-term transformation of agriculture.

Table 12. Effect of EU policies on rural development in the Netherlands

EU policy	Agricultural production	Diversification
Regional	Minor support via Leader	Direct monetary support for rural diversification (e.g. tourism, nature, recreation) via Objective 2, Leader, Interreg, and indirect support through new institutional relationships
Transport	Minor improvement for transport of agricultural goods, disturbance along PBKAL/Betuwelijn routes	Disturbance along PBKAL/Betuwelijn routes
Agriculture	CAP subsidies led to agro-industrial consolidation (milk), but this will decrease after reform	Second pillar CAP provides funds for rural development, including amenities and quality of life in rural areas
Competition	Abolition of import duties made pig farming very profitable in the 1990s; enlarged internal market will generate more opportunities than threats for Dutch farmers in the near future	State aid rules could affect the ability of Dutch government to invest directly in raising the vitality of rural areas; restrictive planning policies may fall under EU scrutiny as well in the future
Environment	Tougher standards for water and soil quality require a reduction of certain kinds of production (pigs) and will stimulate others (especially biomass)	Aid for rural areas linked to sustainable development. Habitat areas mainly in the countryside. Windmill parks and biomass to meet sustainable energy targets
Water	Water quality standards (nitrate) pose a considerable threat to pig and cattle farming	Water policy offers opportunities for integrating water with other functions (housing, nature, recreation)

Table 12 summarises the influences of current EU policy on rural development in the Netherlands, based on the findings of the previous chapters.

This overview shows that regional policy is also important for rural development as a source of finance for restructuring activities. Less than 10 per cent of disposable income in Dutch rural areas is earned in the agricultural agro-industrial sectors (Boekema and van Brussel 2003: 28). Environment, nature and water policies are important because they increasingly impose restrictions on agricultural activities, particularly the economically important greenhouse horticulture and intensive livestock sectors.

Conclusions
In general, European policy has a positive influence on rural development, but the future looks uncertain. The Dutch countryside is very different from rural areas in most other Member States because of the intense pressure for urban development and the intensity of agricultural production; together these present a considerable threat to the landscape, nature and environmental quality. The liberalisation of traditional EU agricultural policy will in time weaken the market support mechanism and force an adjustment to public demands in the areas of environment, nature and animal welfare; this casts doubt on the future of intensive livestock farming in the Netherlands. Dairy and arable farming will have to expand to remain competitive. But can space be found for this? It is questionable whether new forms of multifunctional agriculture will provide a sufficient economic basis for resisting the pressures for urban development, particularly in the western, central and southern regions of the country.

The review of EU rural development policy in 2007 will be highly important for the Netherlands because it may provide an opportunity to obtain a greater share of agricultural funds as a sort of compensation for the expected reduction in the Netherlands' share of traditional agricultural funding. The regional differences in threats and opportunities for rural development appear to be so great as to require an area-based approach to implementing the various measures, based on a spatial vision for rural development (a landscape policy and identification of areas where different types of agriculture can be allowed to develop).

Mainports policy

One of the most important concepts in Dutch spatial planning over the past twenty years is that of the 'mainports': the seaport of Rotterdam and Schiphol Airport. Although the term mainport had been in use in the maritime world for some time, its introduction into the wider policy arena occurred in the early 1980s as the Netherlands was struggling to cope with high unemployment and economic restructuring (van Duinen, forthcoming). During this period it was argued that Schiphol and Rotterdam were the main distribution points in the Netherlands, and thus essential for the country's international competitiveness. This was essentially the reasoning behind central government support for the mainports. With the publication of the Fourth National Policy Document on Spatial Planning in 1989 the institutionalisation of the mainport concept was complete.

Although the mainport concept fell into disfavour by the end of the 1990s (the now defunct Fifth National Policy Document had pushed it to the back burner), it has made a comeback in the new policy document on national spatial planning. The government has already made its standpoint clear in the final text of the spatial planning key decision on the development of the Rotterdam mainport: 'to preserve the strong position of the Netherlands in the global economy and exploit the comparative advantages as much as possible' (Ministerie van V&W et al. 2003: 20).

2. An English summary is available at http://www.havenplan2020.nl/html/engels.html.

Which EU policies affect mainports?
Since mainports are highly sensitive to changes in the global economy, it is of paramount importance to consider the impact of regulatory changes at the European level. The Dutch Government may give equal treatment to both mainports in its policy strategy, but EU policies reflect the fundamental differences between seaports and airports. For this reason, we examine the impacts of EU policy on the Port of Rotterdam and Schiphol Airport separately.

Rotterdam
In the 1980s, global industrial restructuring processes forced Rotterdam, the world's largest port, to rethink its position. It was decided that the port should grow from being primarily a supplier of the German Ruhr area into a major node in an intercontinental network and the gateway for Europe. Although the concept was poorly formulated at the time, it became a rallying cry within the port administration (van Duinen, forthcoming). By the turn of the century, Rotterdam had become a major European centre for trans-shipment, industry, distribution, trade and transport, and the port is an integral part of the logistical chain.

The current thinking about the future of Rotterdam is set out in its strategic plan, Portvision 2020 (*Havenplan 2020*), a follow-up to its *Havenplan 2010*, published about a decade before. The earlier document presented calculations of the amount of extra space needed to support port activities in the future, and led to decisions to build the Betuwelijn and new container terminals and, more recently, the decision to approve the Maasvlakte II port extension. With the problem of capacity largely resolved, the new document concentrates on improving the quality of the port, emphasising accessibility, economic diversification and the environment (Gemeente Rotterdam 2003).[2]

Although the city of Rotterdam has clearly profited from EU regional policy over the past few Structural Funds periods (Objective 2 status and Urban), the port itself has not been so fortunate. Although it did receive some EU support to restructure its former shipbuilding areas, this was mainly to offset the consequences of EU competition policy for state aid. It could be argued that by improving quality of life in the city, EU funding has an indirect positive effect on

Spatial Policy Issues and the EU

those who work in or around the port, and that EU regional policy can help to offset some of the costs of restructuring activities (including, as we shall see below, environmental compensation demanded by the EU for the Maasvlakte II extension). However, for the most part, regional policy has a minimal direct impact on the port, and support from the Structural Funds will probably diminish in future anyway as a result of the enlargement. On a more positive note, funding for research and development under the Lisbon strategy may increase, indirectly benefiting port-related activities.

The port is part of the TEN-T network, the most important element for Rotterdam being the Betuwelijn, which will link the port to the German hinterland. This freight line will also help to shift the model split away from road traffic. Despite its importance for the mainport, the project received TEN status late in the day and the EU is making only a small contribution (see Chapter 'Transport'). Perhaps as important as the Betuwelijn are the various waterway projects that offer opportunities for Dutch shipping companies. The Rhine-Danube link, for example, will open up much of Eastern Europe to Rotterdam, while the newly designated Scheldt-Seine link will expose France to competition from the North. The stimulation of short-sea shipping is also expected to benefit Rotterdam by allowing it to concentrate on larger 'first port of call' transport. At the same time, the award of TEN status to the Iron Rhine (*Ijzeren Rijn*) railway line for freight transport between Rotterdam's rival Antwerp and the German hinterland is a possible threat to the port. Overall, EU transport policy seems to benefit Rotterdam. In particular, the emphasis on alternative modes (rail, water, pipeline) will further strengthen Rotterdam's position compared with its competitors, which are all more dependent on roads (Gemeente Rotterdam, 2003: 58).

In addition to being an important node in the TEN-T network, the Port of Rotterdam is working to enhance its position in the European energy network; an example of this is the construction of an electricity interconnector via an undersea cable between Rotterdam and the UK. The current EU focus on the accession countries and neighbouring regions in TEN-E projects, the liberalisation and harmonisation of energy markets and the discussion on security of supply will provide opportunities for Rotterdam to improve its position in the European energy network.

As stated in the chapter on 'Competition policy', an explicit and long-lasting goal of the EU is to create a true internal market for free but fair competition. In order to achieve this, the EU actively encourages the liberalisation of state companies and the abolition of state aid. To the dismay of Rotterdam, the Netherlands chose to cut subsidies to its shipbuilding industry, while other countries – France and Germany in particular – have continued to provide aid (the Netherlands was rather quick to discontinue aid in general). Although this has been denounced as scandalous by Rotterdam, it may not wish to attract too much attention to itself, considering the public investment now being made (directly and indirectly) in the Maasvlakte II port extension. Besides, Rotterdam will certainly be in a position to exploit the EU enlargement as new markets open up in Eastern Europe (to a large extent open since the early 1990s). The associated increase in the volume of trade will boost port-related activities and could lead to increased demand for Dutch expertise in areas such as dredging, port construction and water management in the accession countries (Bruinsma and Hakfoort 2004). Nevertheless, as the European centre of gravity moves eastwards, Rotterdam will have to guard against possible competition from other areas, especially in Germany, that could serve as distribution nodes.

It has been said that half of the city of Rotterdam will have to be demolished to comply with proposed EU environmental regulations. In fact, nowhere is the impact of EU policy clearer than in the Rijnmond region, where large industrial parks and intensively used transport infrastructure (roads, railways, pipelines and waterways) lie in close proximity to residential neighbourhoods and areas reserved for recreation and nature. The recent controversy over the Maasvlakte II extension into a designated habitat zone (grey dunes, white dunes and shallow sandbanks) is a case in point. The EU has indicated that it considers these activities to be harmful to the habitats in question and the project could only go forward if exemption was granted from the provisions of the Habitats Directive.[3] It was argued that the port of Rotterdam is of vital importance to the Dutch national economy and that the port is an 'essential multimodal node in the TEN-T network' and therefore of community importance as well. A series of mitigation and compensatory measures were proposed, including the construction of 100 ha of new dunes, 10 ha of moist dune valleys and even the designation of 31,250 ha of the North Sea as a nature conservation area (with restrictions on certain disruptive fishing activities). In the end, the Commission agreed to this package, with the proviso that it is kept abreast of progress at defined intervals and receives relevant reports in full. Obviously, the EU will remain watchful of the further development of the port – at the very least to keep a close eye on the habitat compensation. This is all clear evidence that planning is increasingly coming within the sphere of EU policy (Ministerie van V&W et al. 2003).

When the Maasvlakte II is completed, the port of Rotterdam will not need to expand further for some time and the conflict between natural habitats and industrial expansion may lie dormant until around 2020. Other EU environmental rules (e.g. on air, groundwater and soil pollution, safety and noise) will continue to affect the port of Rotterdam, and the Water Framework Directive may influence the prospects for further expansion of port-related activities if this is shown to have negative consequences for water quality. On the positive side, the Mainport Rotterdam Environment Project is considered exemplary by the EU in terms of sustainable development and good governance. Although this does not entail the transfer of large funds, this acknowledgement of best practice may influence other cities, countries or regions to take the same approach. In addition, environmental measures for renewable energy could lead to increased import of biomass via the port of Rotterdam (Gemeente Rotterdam 2003: 48).

3. As stated in the Chapter 'Environment and Nature', this directive prohibits any development that will cause harm to the natural qualities of a designated habitat, unless it is demonstrated to be an urgent matter of public interest (including socioeconomic arguments), in which case compensatory measures must be taken to replace the affected areas and organisms to maintain the cohesion of Natura 2000. However, if a 'priority habitat' is involved – which it was in the case of Rotterdam – stricter rules apply. Here, the project may only be approved in the interests of public health or public safety, or with the explicit approval of the EC.

Schiphol
With over forty million passengers and one million tonnes of cargo transported in 2002, Schiphol is the fourth largest airport in Europe (after London, Paris and Frankfurt). Over the past two decades, passenger numbers have risen rapidly, due mostly to the increased role of the airport as a hub rather than a growth in passenger traffic to and from the Netherlands (currently over 40% of travellers at Schiphol are transfers). Like Rotterdam, Schiphol is easily affected by international developments. The deregulation of the US airline industry in 1978 and its subsequent restructuring affected many European airports: companies became larger and more competitive and air traffic increased worldwide. Like Rotterdam, Schiphol had to rethink its hub and gateway function in the 1980s and reflect on its emergent mainport status. An authoritative report by the Van der Zwan Committee in 1986 argued that Schiphol is important not just for the Amsterdam region, but for the entire nation (van Duinen, forthcoming). This philosophy was reiterated in the Fourth National Policy Document on Spatial Planning and again in the Government's 2000 memorandum on mainport Schiphol: expansion and upgrading of the economic activities in and around Schiphol are of vital importance for the Dutch economy. The current policy seeks to ensure the competitive advantage of the airport and the related positive climate for international businesses, which includes aspects such as good international rail connections, cultural amenities, residential and tax climate and recreation. Not surprisingly, the Schiphol management has wholeheartedly embraced the mainport concept.

With regard to relevant areas of EU policy, we can safely say that regional cohesion policy has a negligible effect on Schiphol. The most important benefit is probably the information and contacts gained through the Interreg II project COFAR (Common Options For Airport Regions). This was set up to investigate common policy options to accommodate the demand for air transport in Western Europe while minimising its impact on land use and the environment (ACI 2003). Although not part of regional policy per se, Schiphol's fifth runway was constructed with a loan from the European Investment Bank. The effect of EU transport policy is also indirect at best, through its support for the PBKAL high-speed rail link. By offering an alternative to European flights, the PBKAL can free up capacity for more lucrative intercontinental flights and make the airport more attractive to passengers travelling to major destinations other than Amsterdam. The reform of EU agricultural policy (abolishing protective price controls) is expected to increase imports of food products, some of which may be carried by air.

Schiphol airport is profoundly affected by EU competition policy. As explained in Chapter 'Competition policy', measures such as the Single European Sky and the Open Skies Agreement are expected to result in further corporate consolidation in the airline industry. The KLM/Air France merger has led to speculation about the position of Schiphol in relation to Paris: it may come to function as the third regional airport of the French capital. This has hidden dangers for the airport: if the airline management decides to reorganise its network to channel the most lucrative routes through France, this could jeopardise the position of Schiphol as a mainport. Competition in Europe is fierce, but EU rules on state aid prohibit governments from assisting their airports, as Belgium recently discovered when it attempted to support its regional airport at Charleroi to secure Ryanair as a carrier. This may serve as a warning to the Netherlands about the limits of its mainports strategy.

Environmental policy is another major factor affecting growth at Schiphol. Expansion is currently being blocked by the imposition of noise zones by the Dutch Government. Because Dutch environmental legislation goes beyond what is required by Brussels, Schiphol is complaining about the lack of a level playing field between European airports. This is illustrated in Table 13.

Table 13. Noise restrictions at European airports

	B	DK	D	F	SU	G	IRL	I	L	**NL**	N	A	P	E	CH	UK	S
Source measures	x	x	x	x						**x**	x	x	x		x	x	x
Spatial planning	x	x	x	x	x	x	x	x	x	**x**	x	x	x	x	x	x	x
Zoning	x	x	x	x	x	x	x	x	x	**x**	x	x	x	x	x	x	x
Fiscal limits on basis of zoning										**x**							
Insulation		x	x	x			x	x		**x**	x	x		x		x	
Noise fees	x	x	x	x				x		**x**	x				x	x	x
Monitoring	x	x	x	x	x			x		**x**	x	x		x	x	x	x

Source: internal memo, Schiphol Airport (2003)

As Table 13 shows, Schiphol does indeed seem to face the most comprehensive package of restrictions in Europe regarding noise pollution. These include rules on the altitude of approach, routes over the sea, holding aircraft that arrive before 6 a.m. if scheduled to arrive later, and operational restrictions for noisy aircraft. Obviously, harmonisation of policy at the EU level would help to create a more level playing field in this respect, and if the EU were to tighten restrictions further, Schiphol would have a head start over other European airports in meeting these requirements.

Table 14. Emissions restrictions at European airports

	Amsterdam	Paris	Frankfurt	Brussels	London	Dublin
Emission norms	x					
Air quality standards (hazardous particles)	x	x	x	x	x	
Odour norm	x					
Exhaust reduction measures	x				x	

Source: internal memo, Schiphol Airport (2003)

Spatial Policy Issues and the EU

As Table 14 shows, Schiphol also seems to be under a stricter regime than its counterparts in terms of emissions standards. For example, Schiphol must not only meet a set of air quality requirements (measured at various points around the airport), but also emission standards for aircraft. The Netherlands is also unique in considering measures to reduce odorous material, and is also one of the few countries in the world (besides Finland, Malaysia and the UK) to consider safety around airports when planning new residential developments. Again, it would benefit Schiphol if the EU were to tighten its emissions restrictions, or incorporate some of the Dutch initiatives into its environmental policy.

Table 15. Effects of EU policies on the two Dutch mainports

EU policy	Port of Rotterdam	Schiphol Airport
Regional	Marginal influence on the port, mainly as by-product of improving liveability (e.g. Interreg III subsidy for river parks)	Negligible effect, some cooperation and information links from an Interreg II project, loan from EIB
Transport	TENs are vital to Rotterdam: Betuwelijn built to link the port to the German hinterland, and various canal projects on the Continent will offer opportunities for Dutch shipping companies; the TEN-E policy can enhance the position of the port in the European energy market	TENs are focused primarily on rail and road transport; this may shift the focus of Schiphol further to intercontinental flights and potentially reduce demand for cargo flights
Agriculture	Relaxation of internal price controls may stimulate further trade from outside the EU	Relaxation of internal price controls may stimulate further trade from outside the EU
Competition	The opening of Eastern European markets offers a wealth of opportunities for the port and poses some threats (Hamburg, Marseille) Support for the mainport may come into conflict with state aid rules, requiring Commission approval	Liberalisation of the airline industry has already led to mergers such as KLM/Air France, with potentially large but unforeseen ramifications
Environment	The Habitats and Birds Directives (Natura 2000) and noise and air pollution directives have already proven a stumbling block for port expansion, and may be so in the future Soil and safety standards could affect prospects for expansion in future	EU rules on acceptable noise and emissions levels could help bring about a level playing field
Water	Water quality standards could affect prospects for expansion in the future	

Conclusions

This chapter has shown that the EU is involved, either directly or indirectly, in the most vital issues of national spatial policy. This involvement, though, is hardly unified: this chapter has repeatedly shown how spatial issues cut across various sectoral EU policies that are dealt with by separate departments.

Both concentrated and diffuse urban development options run up against EU rules. Intensifying urban development in an already densely populated country will soon lead to exceedance of environmental standards, such as those for air and water quality. The capacity for this type of development can be further frustrated by strict EU rules on state aid and public procurement. Ironically, opting for a diffuse pattern of urban development runs counter to the spirit of much of EU policy, but the actual consequences for this are much less severe. The Netherlands may not receive TENs funding for its recent decision to concentrate investment on road rather than rail, but this is no great loss; and it is unlikely to obtain Structural Funds aid for dispersed urban development (where concentration might), but the total funds available for the Netherlands could be much smaller anyway. The strict Natura 2000 rules on flora and fauna apply to both strategies, but especially to the second.

The EU is playing a key role in rural development. The abolition of price controls for agricultural products will act as a catalyst for change because it places farmers at a disadvantage in the short term and propels them towards diversification; environmental controls, especially the Water Framework Directive, will have a similar effect. In the future, agricultural production will remain only in areas where it can weather the storm of the free market, and in other areas will be replaced by more profitable functions (recreation, nature). That the EU supports this is evident from the LIFE fund for Natura 2000, regional cohesion programmes such as Leader+ and converting price controls into income support and rural development funds.

EU policies will have varied and sometimes contradictory consequences for the mainports. Both Schiphol and Rotterdam appear to benefit from the TENs policy, which extends the existing infrastructure networks and creates new distribution opportunities, and the elimination of protected agricultural markets is expected to create more demand for food transport. Competition policy via the Single European Sky has levelled the playing field to the disadvantage of Schiphol and its bilateral arrangements, while the imposition of stricter environmental standards at the EU level will benefit the mainport. For Rotterdam, a reduction of state aid to industry (especially in relation to other Member States) has harmed the mainport, which has seen its expansion efforts frustrated by various environmental directives and the Birds and Habitats Directives.

All this has serious implications for the capacity to draft national policy. Does it make sense, for example, for the Government to draw up a national policy document for Schiphol if it is losing its grip on its future? Or does it make sense to propose a new urban development strategy if this runs counter to current EU policy trends? These are the questions we attempt to answer in the final chapter.

Conclusions

CONCLUSIONS

This study set out to survey the often-hidden presence of the EU in matters of spatial development in the Netherlands. The purpose of this last chapter is to present the findings of each of the sectoral EU policy areas, reflect on the impact of the EU on Dutch planning and explore some of the implications of our findings. Considering the constant evolution of European and national policies and the complexity of the subject matter, this study can just present a snapshot in time. Moreover, in our ambition to survey a wide range of subjects we have had to sacrifice depth for breadth. Recognising this, we present some recommendations for future research to assist others who wish to take up the challenge of investigating the causal relationships indicated in this study. These are summarised in a table at the end of the chapter, along with an indication of urgency, feasibility and availability of data.

Findings

Although the wide scope of our survey did not allow us to demonstrate a causal relationship in quantitative terms, other sources have provided us with a great deal of evidence to support the conclusion that the EU does indeed have an impact on spatial developments. Table 16 presents an overview of our findings; we have chosen to make a distinction between direct and indirect impacts in order to show that a significant proportion of the effects of EU policy are not readily visible in terms of land use, but often work via the planning or development process.

From Table 16, it is clear that each policy area studied at the EU level has both direct and indirect spatial consequences in the Netherlands. Interestingly, the indirect – and therefore usually unseen – consequences are often more significant, and will become increasingly so in the future. Taking regional policy as an example, the physical manifestations of EU investments is rather modest especially if one takes the view that many of these projects may have proceeded without EU aid. The same is true for the TENs in the Netherlands. Citizens may be dimly aware of EU involvement when they see a European flag posted on a sign at a particular construction site, but this disappears as soon as the project is complete. On the negative side, media attention has been given to the frustration of certain developments by European legislation on protected species and by European competition policy. Meanwhile, behind the scenes, the way land is developed in the Netherlands is undergoing more significant structural changes: the 'unseen' component of EU involvement.

In the past decade, the new institutional context posed by the European Union has fundamentally changed the relationship between Member States and their territory, despite the lack of a formal European competency to engage in spatial

Table 16. Direct and indirect impacts of EU policies in the Netherlands

EU policy	Direct spatial impacts	Indirect spatial impacts
Regional cohesion	Rural restructuring (cycle paths, riverbank development, etc.) for tourism and recreation Urban restructuring (Amsterdam Bijlmer, Heerlen station) New business parks (Flevoland, Friesland) New infrastructure (N391 in Drenthe) – All in the form of co-financing	Selective economic development Planning or governance concepts introduced or supported by EU (sustainable development, subsidiarity, additionality) New alliances forged (province/EU via Structural Funds, transnational via Interreg) New data/know-how available (ESPON, framework programmes, Urban, Interreg)
Transport	TEN designation for the PBKAL high-speed railway for passenger transport TEN designation for the Betuwelijn freight railway line from the port of Rotterdam to Germany Maas river project and Iron Rhine in the future – All in the form of co-financing	Areas around stations profit, other areas experience drawbacks Repositioning of port of Rotterdam/Schiphol Airport in transport network as result of new TENs and new short-sea shipping routes Exclusion of Zuiderzeelijn from TEN priority list casts shadow over its viability
Agriculture	Shift to new crops due to loss of production subsidies Concentration of large-scale milk production in North Netherlands Further concentration of intensive cattle farms in Central Netherlands Agricultural areas with a vulnerable natural structure may experience a shift from production to multifunctional agriculture (leisure, recreation, management of natural area)	Shift from EU subsidies for production to income subsidies for farmers and rural restructuring measures can result in new land uses, such as multifunctional agriculture Increased pressure for urban development in rural areas due to reduction in production value Increase in the number of actors and interests in this policy area (CAP second pillar, rural development)
Competition	Free flow of traffic at borders, disappearance of border controls Possible ban on Dutch tax incentives for company headquarters could affect multinational location decisions Liberalisation of air travel sector and advent of small budget airlines departing from regional airports Liberalisation of energy market can affect location decisions for production centres, power lines	Enlarged market areas often stimulate corporate consolidation and specialisation, which can have spatial effects Competition policy can restrict the freedom of governments to conduct economic stimulation policies (e.g. via land pricing) Public procurement rules can affect the implementation of plans Repositioning of border areas from peripheral to transnational nodes (e.g. Arnhem/Nijmegen, Eindhoven/Breda and Maastricht)
Environment and nature	Designated habitat areas can frustrate construction projects Air quality standards can obstruct plans for residential areas New (tougher) noise standards can affect building plans around airports, seaports, highways, etc. Increase in wind parks and reforestation to meet EU green energy objectives	Nature and environment are integrated in the EU approach, but are traditionally separate in Dutch policy Implementation of the Nitrates Directive can endanger the viability of the Dutch livestock sector Strategic environmental assessment raises the evaluation of impacts to a higher level

Water | EU bathing water standards can affect the designation and use of coastal recreation areas | Water Framework Directive can have far-reaching implications for the future of Dutch intensive farming practices
New cross-border cooperation initiatives to achieve WFD objectives can enhance transnational spatial planning

planning. Most of this change is not yet apparent, and usually only becomes manifest in times of direct conflict, as in the case of the Maasvlakte II in Rotterdam or the Grensmaas project on the Belgium border. Sometimes these conflicts play themselves out exclusively at the national level, such as the decision by the Council of State to prohibit an extension to a runway at Eelde airport (because it preferred the EU noise measurement method to the Dutch method). Even more interesting are the potentially far-reaching land use implications of production subsidies, which have transformed the Dutch countryside over the past few decades. By inference, the reform of these policies will have a great effect as well. By changing the rules of the game, vast tracts of land in the west of the Netherlands will be exposed to increased urban pressure, further eroding support for national planning policies based on urban concentration. Similarly, the mainports strategy – one of the cornerstones of national spatial planning policy since the 1980s – has in certain instances been rendered irrelevant by sweeping changes at the European level. The Single European Sky and the liberalisation of the aviation industry (KLM/Air France merger) have profound ramifications for the future of Schiphol, the regional business climate and the Dutch economy. Improved waterway connections on the European continent promoted via the TENs, also 'unseen' in the Netherlands, provide new opportunities for the Port of Rotterdam to maintain or enhance its position in the logistical chain in an enlarged Europe. And while the obligation on Member States to research or map out certain environmental conditions (noise levels, air and water quality) may seem rather benign, these will then be translated into concrete agreements on minimum standards (e.g. the Framework Directive Water) or at the very least be published as benchmarks, drawing negative attention to the counties who fare the worst (e.g. the name and shame method). In conclusion, although it certainly remains necessarily to conduct spatial policy at the national level (if for no other reason than to coordinate EU sectoral policies and integrate it into the planning system), doing so without regard to the growing influence of Brussels will doom it to failure.

Cartographic representation of EU impacts
Clearly, there are plenty of examples of how the EU affects spatial developments in the Netherlands. What is less clear, however, is the combined impact: the EU seems to have a hand in so many different policy areas in so many different ways, making it extremely difficult to get a complete picture, even for the experts. This explains why most studies are limited to a particular sector, region or theme. In an attempt to bring some coherence to our findings, we have compiled a geographical representation of the impacts of EU policies on the territory of the Netherlands (some policies have more effect in certain regions or are in themselves area-based).

Figure 22. Spatial impacts of EU restrictions in the Netherlands

- Natura 2000 conservation areas
- High phosphorus and/or nitrate levels
- Homes possibly within NO_2 exceedance zones
- Project in conflict with EU

Eelde Airport

Maasvlakte 2

Westerschelde Containerterminal

Grensmaas

UNSEEN EUROPE

Spatial impacts of EU investments in the Netherlands

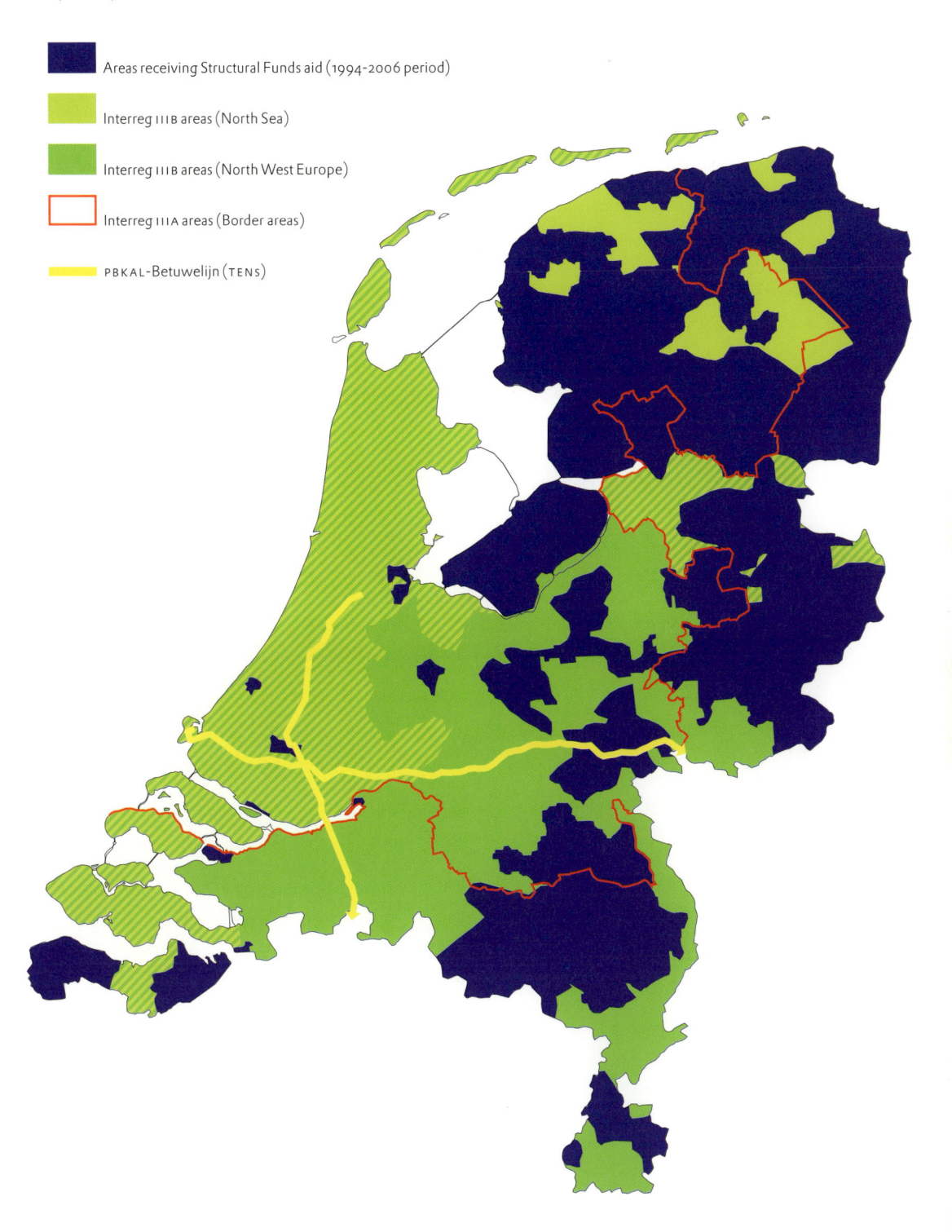

■ Areas receiving Structural Funds aid (1994-2006 period)
■ Interreg IIIB areas (North Sea)
■ Interreg IIIB areas (North West Europe)
□ Interreg IIIA areas (Border areas)
▬ PBKAL-Betuwelijn (TENS)

Conclusions

The incoherence and overlap between the various EU sectoral policies and their impact becomes even more obvious when they are mapped out. Making a distinction between those kinds of policies that seek to stimulate change through investment and subsidies (the carrot approach) and those which impose restrictions (stick) does little to create a more coherent picture: spatially, it remains rather chaotic. Areas receiving Structural Funds (Objective 1 and 2 and Interreg IIIa and IIIb) overlap considerably and do not conform to familiar administrative boundaries.

What these maps do show is that the EU is involved everywhere in the Netherlands. Rural areas seem to experience the most far-reaching consequences of EU policies, however, both in the form of investments (agriculture and Structural Funds) and restrictions (Natura 2000, water policy). EU policies are also extremely important for the future of the two Dutch mainports, especially competition policy, transport and environmental policy, although these are more difficult to depict in terms of land use. The direct effects of EU policies are less pronounced in urban areas, except for the limitations placed on building locations by environmental policy (e.g. air pollution), nature policy and some regional policy support (Objective 2 cities, Urban and Interreg).

Implications

Having indicated the many different ways in which the EU affects spatial developments in the Netherlands, we now look at some of the underlying mechanisms of EU involvement in the spatial development of the Netherlands and reflect on the implications these may have for future spatial developments, planning and administrative relationships.

New administrative relationships
Not only have EU policies affected Dutch spatial development, they have also affected the administrative structures that regulate space. On a number of occasions the Dutch three-tier planning model (national, provincial, municipal) has been upset by the increasing influence of the EU. This is most visible in border regions where the EU has financed cross-border cooperation (Interreg). The new relationships forged between local authorities on different sides of national borders can directly affect land use decisions, for example by linking natural areas and infrastructure and ensuring that land use on one side does not inconvenience spatial goals on the other, or, more indirectly, through the integration of the employment and housing markets. Moreover, the Structural Funds have encouraged certain public sector organisations to work together or do so more intensively; examples include the Nederland-Oost region formed by the provinces of Gelderland and Overijssel and the four main cities united in the G4 lobby in Brussels. Market liberalisation and the splitting up of state-owned companies also creates new administrative relationships, as do the tendering requirements for large projects. Where the EU sometimes takes an active role in the planning process, as in the case of the Maasvlakte II extension to the port of Rotterdam described in the previous chapter, the

European Commission supervises the implementation of compensatory measures.

Non-spatial approach
Since the various sectoral policies analysed in this survey lack an explicit spatial or geographical component, their effects seem somewhat splintered. The Dutch Government is often criticised for its sectoral approach, but this study has shown that the European policy framework is even more sectoral (Schmeitz 2002; Buunk 2003). As stated in Chapter 'Context', the European Union still has no formal competence to conduct spatial policy. The only spatial policy framework at the moment is the informal ESDP, which will become hopelessly outdated after the enlargement in May 2004. At the same time, more and more information about the European territory – and for the first time comparable data – is becoming available from ESPON (see Chapter 'Context'). The final results of the first ESPON programme, which are in the process of being published (2004-2006), will be instrumental for any future EU policy that attempts to transcend sectoral interests with a spatial component, not least because ESPON includes data on the candidate countries as well as Norway and Switzerland.

The possibility of any definitive statement on spatial policy at the EU level is still surrounded by considerable doubt. Although there is a real need to coordinate sectoral policies with a territorial impact, several important developments hang in the balance. One is the enlargement. It is uncertain what sort of input the new Member States would have in a renewed ESDP-like exercise; they could embrace it as a framework for spatial planning on a national or regional scale or as a vehicle to obtain European subsidies. On the other hand, they could also take the view that such an exercise violates the subsidiarity principle. A second unknown factor is territorial cohesion. The recently published Third Cohesion Report has elevated the status of space by defining territorial cooperation as an objective, and the concept of territorial cohesion has been included in the Draft Constitution. Combined with a perceived need to coordinate EU policies within the framework of the Lisbon strategy and the goal of sustainable development, this could potentially lead to the production of a 'European Territorial Cohesion Strategy' with the aim of improving horizontal coordination. However interesting it is to speculate on the prospects for future spatial policy, in whatever form and using whatever terminology, this is outside the scope of our study.

In the absence of an updated ESDP, and given the current document's uncertain status, we can expect the EU to continue to operate, by and large, according to its sectoral modus operandi. For this reason, it is advisable for those involved in spatial policy to keep abreast of developments occurring in the policy sectors investigated in this survey to avoid being caught off-guard by new directives or initiatives. At the same time, a more sectoral orientation can allow actors, such as Dutch planners, to align themselves with important policy areas at the EU level and gain more influence. If this route is taken, it should be pointed out that the EU has a different sectoral organisation than the Netherlands.[1]

---

1. For example, environmental and nature policies are combined in a single department at the EU, but are spread over two ministries in the Netherlands. In addition, the most spatially relevant institution DG Regio, has no direct counterpart in the Dutch national government (its tasks divided largely between the Ministry of Economic Affairs and the Ministry of Housing, Spatial Planning and the Environment).

Even more urgent is the integration of EU sectoral policies in Dutch spatial planning. At the moment, EU regulations continue to be implemented via the national sectors rather than via the extensive spatial planning system. Local authorities are often unaware that certain areas (e.g. habitats) are 'off limits' for building because this has not been included in the regional plan (*streekplan*). These areas can therefore be zoned for development in the local plans. Because of this, developers are sometimes confronted with EU policy after planning permission has already been granted. The various protected areas and restrictions with a clear territorial dimension imposed by the EU should be included in spatial plans as soon as possible in order to avoid confusion, delay and possible obstruction (Verschuuren 2003).

Different cultures of enforcement
In the Netherlands, spatial issues are often resolved in a process of consensus building, involving lengthy consultation procedures and ad-hoc decision making. One consequence is that spatial plans often confirm developments on the ground rather than paving the way for them. Another is that land use planning regulations are not always observed: construction has been more rapid in the 'protected' Green Heart than in the surrounding cities; restrictions on holiday homes have been difficult to enforce; and a significant proportion of building projects are approved via the 'article 19' exemption clause.

At the EU level, in contrast, rules are backed up with clear standards and performance indicators, and strict time schedules and monitoring requirements allow the European Commission to keep an eye on implementation. The Member States are free to decide how they incorporate these rules into their national legislation, but it is the final result that counts. This difference in cultures between the Dutch and European way of dealing with rules can lead to conflict. This was most vividly illustrated by the fact that the Netherlands had to be pressured by the European Court of Justice to introduce stricter regulations for protecting Nature 2000 habitats. Another example is the Nitrates Directive: in a judgement delivered in October 2003, the Dutch Government was ordered to drastically reform its manure regulations, replacing the fee structure with restrictions on use. In short, the European Union does not understand Dutch tolerance. Member States can also be held liable by private parties (such as NGOs) if they fail to live up to EU regulations, including faulty or tardy transposition of EU law into national legislation; in addition, the Court of Justice can fine Member States if a particular standard is not met. The Court of Justice also acts as the final arbiter in the European governance structure, as demonstrated in cases of unwarranted state aid to companies. For some, this is a welcome development: the emphasis placed by Europe on actual implementation and enforcement gives citizens and civil organisations more certainty in their dealings with the government and a sense of fairness, especially if the rules are implemented across Europe. In addition, the binding character of EU directives, even if they originate from sectoral policy, provides an avenue to implement spatial strategies more forcefully than is common in Dutch planning practice.

Coherence between Dutch and EU policy

Besides looking at the areas in which the Dutch and EU policies meet or conflict, it is also interesting to note where the two converge or diverge. Sometimes this is due to a difference in basic philosophy or assumptions regarding political aims and ambitions, and sometimes due to a mismatch in priorities.

In some respects, the Netherlands is the proverbial 'teacher's pet'. Together with Britain, the Netherlands is top of the class in the liberalisation of state-owned companies and abolition of state aid. The Dutch and the EU are also eye-to-eye on agricultural reform: both favour more liberalisation, elimination of production support, linking income support to farmers with environmental and animal welfare standards and the promotion of rural development. Water, environmental and nature policy, though, are a different matter altogether: the Netherlands has been finding it hard to incorporate certain directives into national legislation fully and on time. This was the case for Natura 2000, and it is quite likely that the Dutch may request a deferment or special exemption for the Nitrates Directive, the Water Framework Directive and the Air Quality Framework Directive; the spatial aspect is certainly a complicating factor here. Having once taken the lead in drafting these policies, the Netherlands may be having some misgivings now they actually have to be implemented.

Another interesting case of recent policy divergence is transport. Here, the EU explicitly favours rail transport, whereas the latest Dutch transport policy includes a host of road and waterway improvements, but no additions to the rail network. The recent decision to complete the A4 motorway link in Midden-Delfland is accompanied by a budget for the infrastructure costs (at least at the time of writing), but not for nature compensation as originally intended. The Netherlands also takes a different approach to regional economic development, partly abandoning the European regional policy objective of reducing disparities in favour of a policy of concentrating resources in areas with economic potential, such as mainports. Through the Structural Funds, the EU has encouraged the Netherlands to invest in weak regions again, but after 2007 it is unclear whether the country will continue in this direction or return to the standpoint articulated in the Fourth National Policy Document on Spatial Planning. If it follows the latter course, in the face of opposition from 'weak' regions, the Netherlands will have to define and quantify what 'economic potential' is and how support for these areas will create more wealth. In any case, it is practically unthinkable that the ex-Objective 1 province of Flevoland will receive any economic development aid in the foreseeable future.

Recommendations for further research

The main purpose of this study was to examine the various ways in which Dutch spatial developments are affected by policy set at the European level. As this was an exploratory study, the emphasis was on identifying possible causal links rather than actually proving they exist. The latter was also not feasible

given the broad scope of the research. We hope that others will be inspired by
the relationships we have uncovered and subject them to more thorough and
rigorous investigation. At the end of each policy chapter, we indicated whether
or not we felt that this would be a fruitful area for further in-depth research;
these findings are summarised in Table 17.

Table 17. Potential for future research

	Policy relevance	Availability of relevant information/data	Ease of establishing a cause–effect relationship
Regional policy	+	++	+
Transport	+	++	++
Agriculture	+++	+++	+
Internal market	++	+	+
Environment	+++	+++	+++
Water	++	++	+

Regional policy
Regional policy has obvious and visible spatial impacts (infrastructure
development, business parks, etc.) but it is very difficult to establish a
cause–effect relationship. Moreover, it is not entirely credible that all projects
carried out under the banner of regional policy do indeed meet the
additionality criteria; and the fact that they are only co-financed by the EU also
raises the question of how much can be ascribed to European investment.

For the current period (2000–2006) a number of midterm reviews are
becoming available in the Netherlands which could be used as research aids.
However, these studies address the economic effect of EU regional policy (i.e.
the creation of jobs) and not the spatial effects; any further in-depth research
will have to read between the lines to discover the spatial impacts. Another
avenue is to compare old spatial plans (prior to EU programme designation)
and establish through interviews with key players whether the change was in
fact caused by the award of EU funds. Additional quantitative data on the
impact of the Structural Funds in the EU and candidate countries will become
available from ESPON (programmes 2.2.1 and 2.2.2) by the end of 2004.

The Third Cohesion Report defines the rules of the game for receiving funding
after 2006. As expected, the Netherlands will not be eligible for solidarity
funds (Objective 1), but could benefit from economic competitiveness and
especially territorial cooperation. Participation in these EU programmes is
bound to influence spatial developments to some extent.

Transport
So far, the TENs policy has had little perceptible direct effect in the
Netherlands: both the PBKAL and Betuwelijn projects would have gone ahead
anyway, and no routes were changed and no new initiatives taken on account
of the EU. The TENs are primarily international connections and any research
should focus on this aspect. There are several ongoing projects doing exactly

this, including research by NEA, ESPON and TNO-Inro (Institute for Traffic and Transport, Logistics and Spatial Development). Some interesting connections with logistics can be made.

Our finding that the indirect impact of European transport policy is crucial to the development of the two Dutch mainports certainly warrants further in-depth research. This would ideally include the influence of other aspects of EU policy, such as competition and the environment, on the position of these strategic locations in European and global distribution networks.

Agriculture
EU agricultural policy has left a significant imprint on the Dutch landscape, and will continue to do so in future, even in the absence of production subsidies. Most current Dutch research pays little attention to the spatial aspects, even though these are considerable. In the near future ESPON will publish its findings on agriculture (programme 2.1.3), and these can be worked out further for the Netherlands. Special attention can be paid to the effect of rural development policies in the Dutch context and the question of whether a more territorial or area-based policy approach would be more effective than the current approach.

Competition/internal market
The internal market has many indirect influences on spatial developments in the Netherlands, but causal links that go beyond anecdotal evidence are difficult to establish. This will complicate any further research that goes beyond surveying the various ways that the Dutch Government and local authorities has come into conflict with the EU's attempts to regulate the internal market. On the other hand, considering that the relationship between competition policy and spatial development is not well researched, this can be seen as an opportunity for pioneering research. Particularly the subject of policy conflicts with regional or environmental policy sectors appears promising. Another interesting topic is to monitor the spatial effects of liberalisation, which are potentially large, but cannot be easily traced back to EU policy. Finally, the influence of the expanded market (i.e. free flow of labour, goods and capital) will be of great concern to Dutch businesses, particularly at or near the mainports, and this can have large indirect spatial consequences. The degree to which EU citizens avail themselves of the opportunity to live and work abroad, and the territorial consequences this may have is another interesting research topic.

Environment and Nature
This is obviously a very fruitful topic for future research into the territorial impact of EU policies in the Netherlands. A useful approach would be to map the spatial implications of regulations on noise, water and air quality, safety zones and the spatial consequences of the EU's sustainable energy policy. If superimposed on a map of the protected habitats areas, this would provide a comprehensive overview that could be used to identify areas of conflict with proposed future urban development. Another useful topic is the incorporation

of new environmental regulations, including Strategic Environmental Assessment, into Dutch spatial planning legislation and practice.

Water
The EU policy on water has a spatial impact and is already being researched by organisations such as the National Institute for Public Health and the Environment (RIVM), the National Institute for Inland Water Management and Wastewater Treatment (RIZA) and the National Institute for Coastal and Marine Management (RIKZ), but the spatial aspect is not always explicit. Alterra's survey of the spatial effects of the Water Framework Directive in the Netherlands received considerable attention in the media and policy circles. Future research could focus on the following questions: Are EU instruments sufficient for spatial interventions? Which spatial, sectoral and technical measures can reconcile agricultural production and water quality? And what are the consequences for border regions?

LITERATURE

Airports Council International (2003), *ACI Europe guide to finance instruments for European airports*, October, Airports Council International.

Asbeek Brusse, W., J. Bouma & R.T. Griffiths (2002), *De toekomst van het europees gemeenschappelijk landbouwbeleid. Actuele vraagstukken en perspectieven voor Nederland*, Utrecht: Lemma.

Bieleman, J. (1992), *Geschiedenis van de landbouw in Nederland: veranderingen en verscheidenheid*, Boom. Meppel / Amsterdam.

Blom, W.F., H.S.M.A. Diederen, R.J.M. Folkert & K. van Velze (2003), *Notitie NO_2-aandachtspunten rond snelwegen in 2010 en 2015 in Nederland*, Bilthoven: Milieu- en Natuurplanbureau.

Boiten, E. & S. van der Sluis (2000), 'Ruimtelijke effecten van Europees beleid', in: Eijndhoven (ed.), *Ruimtelijk beleid in Europese context*, The Hague: Rathenau Instituut.

Bolsius, E., J. Groen, L. van Aarsen, Y. van Bentum, F. Bethe, P. Smeets en M. Wijermans (1997), *Landelijke gebieden in Europa: eindrapport studieproject*, The Hague: Rijksplanologische Dienst.

Bolt, F. van der, R. Van den Bosch, T. Brock, P. Hellegers, C. Kwakernaak, D. Leenders, O. Schuurmanns & P. Verdonschot (2003), *Aquarein. Gevolgen van de Europese kaderrichtlijn Water voor landbouw, natuur, recreatie en visserij*, Alterra-rapport 835, Wageningen: Alterra.

Bont, C.J.A.M. de, J.F.M. Helming & J.H. Jager (2003), *Hervorming gemeenschappelijk Landbouwbeleid 2003, Gevolgen van de voorstellen van de Europese Commissie voor de Nederlandse landbouw*, The Hague: LEI.

Bosma, Jelte & Judith van Dijk (2003), 'Stroomgebiedvisies en waterkansenkaarten: nieuwe instrumenten in het waterbeleid', in: Hidding, Marjan & Maarten van der Vlist (eds.), (2003), *Ruimte en water: planningsopgaven voor een rode delta,* Den Haag: Sdu Uitgevers.

Bruinsma, F., M. Koetse, P. Rietveld & R. Vreeker (2002), 'Social costs of direct and indirect land use by transport infrastructure', *European Journal of Transport and Infrastructure Research* 2(2): 73-93.

Bruinsma, W. & J. Hakfoort (2004), 'The economic effects of the enlargement of the European Union for the Netherlands', in: W. Bruinsma, J. Hakfoort and E. Wever (2004), *The regional impact of enlargement of the European Union,* Assen: Van Gorcum.

Buunk, W.W., Hans Hetsen & Anton J. Jansen (1999), 'From sectoral to regional policies: a first step towards spatial planning in the European Union?', *European Planning Studies* 7(1): 81-99.

Buunk, W.W. (2003), *Discovering the locus of European integration. The contribution of planning to European governance in the cases of Trans European Networks, Structural Fund programmes, Natura 2000 and Agri-Environmental measures*, Nijmegen: University of Nijmegen.

Buuren, P.J.J. van (2003), 'De Reconstructiewet concentratiegebieden', *Milieu en Recht* 30(5): 146-151.

Cammen, Hans van der & Len De Klerk (2003), *Ruimtelijke Ordening: van Grachtengordel tot Vinexwijk*, Utrecht/Antwerpen: Het Spectrum.

CBS (2003), *Statistisch Jaarboek 2003*, Voorburg: Centraal Bureau voor de Statistiek.

Commissie Integraal Waterbeheer [Commission for Integrated Water Management] (2002), *Water in Beeld 2002: voortgangsrapportage over het waterbeheer in Nederland*, Den Haag: Commissie Integraal Waterbeheer/CUWVO.

Committee on Spatial Development (1999), *European Spatial Development Perspective*, Luxembourg: European Commission.

CPB [Netherlands Bureau for Economic Policy Analysis] (2003), *Competition on European Energy Markets,* Centraal Planbureau document no. 33, The Hague: Centraal Planbureau.

Dam, F. van, M. Jókòvic, A. van Hoorn & S. Heins (2003), *Landelijk wonen*, Den Haag/Rotterdam: Ruimtelijk Planbureau/NAi Uitgevers.

Diaw, K. & J. Gorter (2002), *The remedy may be worse than the disease: a critical account of the Code of Conduct*, CPB Discussion Paper 5, The Hague: Centraal Planbureau.

Didde, René (2000), 'Bedreigde dieren rukken op: Europese natuurbeschermingsregels frustreren bouwplannen', *Binnenlands Bestuur* 21(39): 24–25.

Duinen, L. van (forthcoming), *Planning Imagery: the emergence and political acceptance of planning concepts in Dutch national planning*, PhD Thesis, University of Amsterdam.

Eck, W. van, A. van den Ham, A.J. Reinhard, R. Leopold & K.R. de Poel (2002), *Ruimte voor landbouw, uitwerking van vier ontwikkelingsrichtingen*, Wageningen: Alterra.

Ecorys (2003), *Mid Term Review Kompas voor het Noorden*, Ecorys Research and Consulting, Regionale & Stedelijke Ontwikkeling, Luc Boot, Manfred Wienhoven and Atze Verkennis, 13 mei 2003.

Ederveen, S., H. de Groot & R. Nahuis (2002), *Fertile soil for Structural Funds?*, CPB Discussion Paper 10, The Hague: Centraal Planbureau.

Elbertsen, J.W.H., P.F.M. Verdonschot, B. Roels & J.G. Hartholt (2003), *Definitiestudie Kaderrichtlijn Water (KRW), 1. Typologie Nederlandse Oppervlaktewateren*, Alterra rapport 669, Wageningen: Alterra.

ERAC [European Regional Affairs Consultants] (2003), *Analyse effecten structuurfondsprogramma's in Nederland: periode 1994–1999*, with IPO, PMN, UvT.

ESPON [European Spatial Planning Observatory Network] (2003), *Transport Services and Networks,* Third interim report of ESPON, project 1.2.1, August 2003.

European Commission (1999), *The Customs Policy of the European Union*, Luxembourg: European Communities.

European Commission (2000), *Competition Policy in Europe and the Citizen*, Luxembourg: European Communities.

European Commission (2001a), *Working for the Regions,*. Luxembourg: European Communities.
European Commission (2001b), *Concurrentiekracht en de kwaliteit van leven: Een bloemlezing van projecten in de Benelux, gefinancierd door de Structuurfondsen*, Luxembourg: European Communities.
European Commission (2001c), *White Paper European transport policy for 2010: Time to Decide,* Luxembourg: European Communities.
European Commission (2001d), *Sixth Environmental Action Programme, Environment 2010: Our future, Our choice,* Luxembourg: European Communities.
European Commission (2002a), *The Programming of the Structural Funds 2000-2006: an Initial Assessment of the Urban Initiative,* COM(2002), 308 final, Luxembourg: European Communities.
European Commission (2002b), *Trans-European Transport Network:* TEN-T *priority projects*, Luxembourg: European Communities.
European Commission (2002c), *It's a better life: How the EU's single market benefits you.* Luxembourg: European Communities.
European Commission (2002c), *Structural Policies and European Territory: Cooperation without Frontiers,* Luxembourg: European Communities.
European Commission (2002d), *Implementing the Internal Energy Market: First Benchmarking Report,* Luxembourg: European Communities.
European Commission (2003a), *Europa in Nederland: Regionale steun van de Europese Unie aan Nederland,* Factsheet, Juli 2003, Luxembourg: European Communities.
European Commission (2003b), *A European Initiative for Growth: Investing in Networks and Knowledge for Growth and Jobs,* COM(2003), 690 final, Luxembourg: European Communities.
European Commission (2003c), *State Aid Scoreboard: Spring 2003 update 22,* COM(2003), 225 final, Luxembourg: European Communities.
European Commission (2003d), *Second progress report on economic and social cohesion*, Luxembourg: European Communities.
European Commission (2003e), *2003 Environment Policy Review,* COM(2003), 745 final. Luxembourg: European Communities.
European Commission (2003f), *Mid-term Review of the Common Agriculture Policy,* Luxembourg: European Communities.
European Commission (2004a), *A New Partnership for Cohesion: Third Report on Economic and Social Cohesion*, Luxembourg: European Communities.
European Commission (2004b), *Building our Common Future: Policy challenges and budgetary means of the Enlarged Union 2007–2013,* Com(2004), 101 final, Luxembourg: European Communities.
European Court of Justice (2002), *European Commission versus Ireland regarding Directives 79/409/EEC and 92/43/EEC, Case No.* C-117/00, 13 June 2002.
Evers, David (2002), 'Towards an Abolition of National Retail Planning in the Netherlands', *Tijdschrift voor Sociale en Economische Geografie* 93(1): 107–113.
Expertisecentrum LNV (2003a), *Boeren op pad naar vrijhandel,* Nr. 2003/203, Ede: Expertisecentrum LNV.

Expertisecentrum LNV (2003b), *Vrijhandel, milieu, natuur en landschap*, Nr. 2003/226, Ede: Expertisecentrum LNV.

Faludi, A. & A. van der Valk (1994), *Rule and Order: Dutch Planning Doctrine in the Twentieth Century*, Dordrecht: Kluwer.

Faludi, A. & B. Waterhout (2002), *The Making of the European Spatial Development Perspective – No Masterplan*, London: Routledge

Faludi, A. & W. Zonneveld (1998a), *Europese integratie en de Nederlandse ruimtelijke ordening*. WRR voorstudie nr. 102, The Hague: Sdu Uitgevers.

Faludi, A. & W. Zonneveld (1998b), 'Shaping Europe: the European Spatial Development Perspective', *Built Environment* 23(4): 257-314.

Faludi, Andreas, ed. (2002), *European Spatial Planning*, Lincoln Institute of Land Policy, Cambridge, MA.

Fleurke, F. & J.R. Hulst (2002), *Europees ruimtelijk beleid en het bestuurlijk stelsel voor de ruimtelijke ordening*, The Hague: DG Ruimte, Ministerie van VROM.

Freriks, A.A., T. Peters, J. Robbe & J.M. Verschuuren (2002), *De invloed van het Europees recht op het Ruimtelijk bestuursrecht*, Publicatie van de Vereniging voor Bouwrecht, nr. 30. Deventer: Kluwer.

Gemeente Rotterdam (2003), *Havenplan 2020: ruimte voor kwaliteit*. Concept ontwerp havenplan, december 2003, Rotterdam.

Gordijn, H., F. Verwest and A. & Hoorn (2003a), *Energie is ruimte*, Den Haag/Rotterdam: Ruimtelijk Planbureau/NAi Uitgevers.

Gordijn, H., W. Derksen, J. Groen, H. Pálsdóttir, M. Piek, N. Pieterse & D. Snellen (2003b), *De ongekende ruimte verkend*, Den Haag/Rotterdam: Ruimtelijk Planbureau/NAi Uitgevers.

Hajer, M.A. (2000), 'Transnational Networks as Transnational Policy Discourse', pp. 135-142 in: W. Salet and A. Faludi, *The Revival of Strategic Spatial Planning*. Amsterdam: KNAW.

Hamsvoort, C.P.C.M. van der, G.B.C. Backus, P. Berkhout, C. van Bruchem, G. Mighels, P. Salz, A.B. Smit & A.K. van der Werf (2002), *Trendverkenningen Nederlandse landbouw, een bundel essays ten behoeve van de tweede Natuurverkenning*, Planbureaustudies nr. 4, Natuurplanbureau, Wageningen.

Heijmerink, R. (2002), 'De provincie Noord-Brabant en internationalisering in de Ruimtelijke Ordening', *Tijdschrift voor omgevingsrecht* 2(4): 137-142.

High Level Group (2003), *High Level Group on the Trans-European Transport Network*, Report, Chair Van Miert, 27 June.

Janssen, John A.M. & Joop H.J. Schaminée (2003), *Europese Natuur in Nederland: Habitattypen*, Utrecht: KNNV-Uitgeverij.

Klinge-van Rooij, I., B.F.C. Boot, M. Fokkema, M.E. Jansen & T.T. van Kreij (2003), *Bouwen voor Ruimte: Europese richtlijnen en verdragen*, Deventer: Kluwer.

Kol, J. (2001), 'Waarheen met de Europese landbouw?', *Internationale Spectator* 55(9): 440-446.

Koppert, A.J. (2001), 'Voortgang ontwerp EU-richtlijn omgevingsgeluid', *Geluid*, juli: 101-102.

Kusiak, L. (1997), 'Overlast en schade door Europees goederenvervoer zijn alarmerend: nationale belangen zitten milieuvriendelijke aanpak in de weg', ROM magazine 15(9): 14-17.

Lijzen, J.P.A. & A. Ekelenkamp (1995), *Bronnen van diffuse bodembelasting*, 950011007, RIVM, Bilthoven.

Louwers, R. (2003), 'Europese Schatkist', VROM.NL 5(5): 1-8.

Massink, H. & G. Meester (2002), *Boeren bij vrijhandel*, Den Haag: Ministerie van LNV.

Meinardi, C.R. (2003), *Het Nederlandse grondwater; de indeling in grondwaterlichamen en een aanzet voor een conceptueel model voor de karakterisering*, RIVM intern rapport, Bilthoven: RIVM.

Meinardi, C.R., M.S.M. Groot & H.F. Prins (2003), *basiswaarden voor spoorelementen in het zoete grondwater van Nederland: gegevens uit de landelijke en provinciale meetnetten (LMG, PMG, LMB, sprengen Veluwe)*, RIVM rapport 714801028, Bilthoven: RIVM.

Milieu- en Natuurplanbureau (2001), *Milieucompendium 2001*, Alphen aan den Rijn: Kluwer. [English summary available at: http://www.rivm.nl/bibliotheek/digitaaldepot/030612sueb2003.pdf]

Milieu- en Natuurplanbureau (2003a), *Milieubalans 2003*, Alphen aan den Rijn: Kluwer.

Milieu- en Natuurplanbureau (2003b), *Milieucompendium 2003*, Alphen aan den Rijn: Kluwer.

Minderhoud, F. (1997), 'Europees infrastructuurbeleid en de gevolgen voor natuur en milieu', *Idee* 18(2): 16-19.

Ministerie van BZ (2002), *Staat van de Europese Unie,* September 2002, The Hague: Ministry of Foreign Affairs.

Ministerie van BZ (2003), *Staat van de Europese Unie*, September 2003. The Hague: Ministry of Foreign Affairs.

Ministerie van LNV (1995), *Dynamiek en Vernieuwing* [Change and Renewal], The Hague: Ministry of Agriculture, Nature Management and Fisheries.

Ministerie van LNV (2001), *Plattelandsontwikkelingsprogramma Nederland ter invulling van verordening (EG), nr. 1257/1999 van de Raad, van 17 mei 1999*, POP Nederland, The Hague: Ministry of Agriculture, Nature Management and Fisheries.

Ministerie van V&W [Ministry of Transport, Public Works and Water management], Ministerie van VROM [Ministry of Spatial Planning, Housing and the Environment], Ministerie van Financiën [Ministry of Finance], Ministerie van EZ [Ministry of Economic Affairs], Ministerie van LNV [Ministry of Agriculture, Nature and Food Quality] (2003), *Definitieve tekst PKB-plus Project Mainportontwikkeling Rotterdam, Deel 4,* September 2003, The Hague.

Ministerie van VROM (1991), *Fourth Report on Spatial Planning Extra,* The Hague: Ministry of Spatial Planning, Housing and the Environment.

Ministerie van VROM (1999), *Ruimtelijke Perspectieven in Europa.* Rijksplanologische Dienst (RPD), The Hague: Ministry of Spatial Planning, Housing and the Environment.

Ministerie van VROM (2001a), *Vierde Nationaal Milieubeleidsplan* [Fourth National Environmental Policy], Den Haag: Ministry of Spatial Planning, Housing and the Environment.

Ministerie van VROM (2001b), *Fifth Report on Spatial Planning*, The Hague: Ministry of Spatial Planning, Housing and the Environment.

Ministerie van VROM, (2002), *Brief van Staatssecretaris van VROM aan de Tweede Kamer van 21 oktober 2003*, The Hague: Ministry of Spatial Planning, Housing and the Environment.

Mooij, Ruud A. de & Richard Nahuis (2003), 'Kansen en bedreigingen van de EU-uitbreiding', *Tijdschrift voor Politieke Geografie* 24(3): 3-29.

Mooij, Ruud de and Paul Tang (2003), *Four Futures of Europe*, The Hague: Centraal Planbureau.

Moseley, Malcolm J. (2003), *Rural Development, principles and practice*, Thousand Oaks, CA: Sage Publications.

NEA (2003), TEN-STAC: *Scenarios, traffic forecasts and analysis of corridors on the Trans-European Network, Description of the base year 2000 and interim forecasts 2020*, NEA Research and Training BV.

Netherlands Scientific Council for Government Policy (1992), *Ground for choices, four perspectives for the rural areas in the European Community*, Report to the Government No. 42, The Hague: SDU Publishers.

Peters, D. (2003), 'Cohesion, Polycentricity, Missing links and bottlenecks: Conflicting spatial storylines for pan-European transport investments', *European Planning Studies* 11(3): 317-339.

Pieterse, N.M., T. Casimir & F. Kwadijk (2002), *Grondwaterbescherming Utrechtse Heuvelrug, handvatten voor actieve bescherming van de grondwaterkwaliteit*, Deel 2: visie, Grontmij rapport 13/99031120/NP.

Ploeg, J. D, van der, A. Long & J. Banks (2002), *Living Countrysides*, Doetinchem: Elsevier.

Raad voor Verkeer & Waterstaat (2003), *Logistieke uitdagingen voor de Nederlandse economie*, juni 2003.

Redeker, N. (2002), 'Uitbreiding: een andere Unie vereist een andere solidariteit: noodzaak van een nieuw Europees structuur- en cohesiebeleid' *Internationale Spectator,* December: 591-595.

Richardson, T. & O. Jensen (2000), 'Discourses of Mobility and Polycentric Development: A Contested View of European Spatial Planning', *European Planning Studies* 8(4): 503-520.

Robert, J., M.A. Figueiredo, M. Hollanders, C.J. Reincke, T. Stumm & J.M. de Vet (2001), *Spatial impacts of Community policies and costs of non-coordination*, Study carried out at the request of the Directorate-General Regional Policy, European Commission, ERDF contract 99.00.27.156.

Rooij, R.A.A. de (2003), *Nederlandse gemeenten en provincies in de Europese Unie. Gevolgen van het nationale EU-lidmaatschap voor subnationale overheden*, Dordrecht: Kluwer.

Ruijgrok, W. & J.J. Erbrink (2000), *Invloed van Europese beleidstrends op bio-energie in Nederland*, KEMA Nederland, Utrecht: Novem Publicatiecentrum.

Sambeek, E.J.W. van, E. van Thuijl & C.J. Roos (2003), *De Europese context van het Nederlandse duurzame elektriciteitsbeleid*, May 2003, The Hague: RIVM.

Scharpf, Fritz (1999), *Governing in Europe: Effective and Democratic,* Oxford: Oxford University Press.
Schendelen, Rinus van (2002), *Machiavelli in Brussels: the Art of Lobbying the EU,* Amsterdam: Amsterdam University Press.
Schmeitz, Peter (2002), 'Wat is territoriale cohesie? Op weg naar een Europees ruimtelijk ontwikkelingsbeleid', *Tijdschrift voor omgevingsrecht* 2(5): 174–177.
SER [Social and Economic Council] (2003), *Naar een doeltreffender, op duurzaamheid gericht EU-landbouwbeleid,* SER-advies nr. 7, The Hague: SER.
Strijker, Dirk (2003), 'Brussel en het Nederlandse platteland', in: Boekema, F. & J. van Brussel (eds.), *Theoretische en empirische aspecten van plattelandsvernieuwing,* Maastricht: Shaker Publishing.
TCB [Technische Commissie Bodembescherming] (2001), *Aanzet voor stroomgebiedenbeheer,* Advies, The Hague.
Terluin, Ida J. & G.S. Venema (2003), *Towards regional differentiation of rural development policy in the EU,* The Hague: Agriculture Economics Research Institute (LEI).
Tewdwr-Jones, M. & R.H. Williams (2001), *The European Dimension of British Planning,* London: Spon press.
Tweede Kamer (2002), EU *Structuurfondsen,* brief aan de Tweede Kamer van de Staatssecretaris van economische Zaken, TK 27813, nr. 4, oktober 2002.
Vereijken, P.H. (2002), 'Ruimteheffing in natura', ESB *Economisch statistische berichten,* 87, 15 februari: 132-134.
Verschuuren, J.M. (2003), 'De invloed van het Europees recht op het Ruimtelijk bestuursrecht', *Bouwrecht* 40(7): 545-571.
Vet, J.M. de & K.-J. Reincke (2002), 'Ruimtelijke samenhang van Europees sectorbeleid: een majeur afstemmingsprobleem', *Tijdschrift voor omgevingsrecht* 2(2): 55–59.
Vickerman, R., K. Spiekerman & M. Wegener (1999), 'Accessibility and economic development in Europe', *Regional studies* 33(1): 1-15.
Waterhout, B. (2002), *De machteloze ruimtelijke planner in Europa,* Paper ten behoeve van Plandag 2002, Dordrecht, 6 Juni.
Willems, W.J., B. Fraters, C.R. Meinardi, H.F.R. Reinders & C.G.E.M. van Beek (2002), *Nutriënten in bodem en grondwater: kwaliteitsdoelstellingen en kwaliteit 1984–2000,* RIVM rapport 718201004, Bilthoven: RIVM.
Williams, R.H. (1996), *European Union Spatial Policy and Planning,* London: Paul Chapman Publishing.
Woestenburg, M. & G. van Duinhoven (2002), 'De Europese Commissie is geen boeman: trots op mooie natuur als leidraad voor uitvoering van Europese natuurwetgeving', *Landwerk* 3(6): 10-13.
Woude, A.M. van der (1992), 'De toekomst van de West-Europese landbouw', *Spil* 5: 53-59

LIST OF INTERVIEWEES

Berg-MacGillivray, Margreet van den (Ministry of Agriculture, Nature and Food Quality, LNV),
Brand, Petra van den (Ministry of Agriculture, Nature and Food Quality, LNV),
Bruinsma, Willy (Ministry of Economic Affairs, EZ),
Buntsma, Joost (Ministry of Transport, Public Works and Water Management, V&W),
De Bruijn, Henk (Port of Rotterdam),
Dekker, Resianne (Port of Rotterdam),
Duinen, Lianne van (Amsterdam Study Centre for the Metropolitan Environment, AME),
Eijkeren, Rob van (House of the Dutch Provinces in Brussels),
Faludi, Andreas (University of Nijmegen),
Hartkamp, Justus (Schiphol Group),
Haverkate, Roel (Province of Drenthe),
Heest, Jan van (Permanent Representation of the Netherlands to the EU),
Hidding, Marjan (Wageningen University and Research Centre),
Hobus, Wim (Province of Gelderland),
Lauwerijssen, Janneke (Ministry of Economic Affairs, EZ),
Kranenburg, Wim (Schiphol Group),
Lont, Alexander (planner in the northern Netherlands),
Massink, Henk (Ministry of Agriculture, Nature and Food Quality, LNV),
Mesker, August (Confederation of Netherlands Industry and Employers, VNO/NCW),
Ploeg, Wim (Ministry of Transport, Public Works and Water Management),
Pluckel, Hans (Association of the Provinces, IPO),
Rabbinge, Rudy (Wageningen University and Research Centre),
Remmers, Monique (Ministry of Agriculture, Nature and Food Quality, LNV),
Rijkhoff, Jos (Confederation of Netherlands Industry and Employers, VNO/NCW),
Schmeitz, Peter (Ministry of Spatial Planning, Housing and the Environment, VROM),
Smits, Simon J.H. (Permanent Representation of the Netherlands to the EU),
Verdonk, Hans (G4 office in Brussels),
Vermuë, Albert (Ministry of Agriculture, Nature and Food Quality, LNV),
Verspoor, Hans (Ministry of Spatial Planning, Housing and the Environment, VROM),
Waterhout, Bas (Research Institute for Housing, Urban and Mobility Studies, OTB),
Zonneveld, Wil (Research Institute for Housing, Urban and Mobility Studies, OTB)

ABOUT THE AUTHORS

David Evers studied political science in Portland, Oregon (Reed College). At the University of Amsterdam he completed a broad MA programme in the social sciences, followed by an MA in town and country planning. In 2004 he finished his PhD research on location policy for out-of-town shopping malls in North-West Europe, which also is his specialisation at the Netherlands Institute for Spatial Research.

Nico van Ravesteyn studied law. Until 2002 he worked as deputy director for Spatial Policy Research at the Ministry of Spatial Planning, Housing and the Environment. At present he is deputy director at the Netherlands Institute for Spatial Research, where he is concerned with international contacts.

COLOFON

Research
Nico van Ravesteyn (project manager)
David Evers
Nico Pieterse

Aldert de Vries, Anton van Hoorn, Lia van den Broek, Marnix Breedijk and Restlan Aykaç provided much appreciated support.

Dr Wil Zonneveld (OTB, Delft) and Peter Schmeitz (Ministry VROM) provided may useful comments on draft versions of this report.

Illustrations
David Evers in co-operation with TI&OSM

Copy Editing
Derek Middleton, text compilation – editing – translation

Design
Typography Interiority & Other Serious Matters, The Hague

Printing
Die Keure, Brugge (Belgium)

© 2004 NAi Publishers, Rotterdam. All right reserved. No part of this publication may be reproduced, stored in a retrieval system, or transmitted in any form or by any means, electronic, mechanical, photocopying, recording or otherwise, without the prior written permission of the publisher.

For works of visual artists affiliated with a CISAC-organisation the copyrights have been settled with Beeldrecht in Amsterdam
© 2004, c/o Beeldrecht Amsterdam

It was not possible to find all the copyright holders of the illustrations used. Interested parties are requested to contact NAi publishers, Mauritsweg 23, 3012 JR Rotterdam, The Netherlands.
NAi publishers is an internationally orientated publisher specialized in developing, pruducing and distributing books on architecture, visual arts and related disciplines.
www.naipublishers.nl
info@naipublishers.nl

Available in North, South, and Central America through D.A.P./Distributed Art Publishers Inc, 155 Sixth Avenue 2nd Floor, New York, NY 10013-1507,
tel +1 212 627 1999, fax +1 212 627 9484,
dap@dapinc.com

Available in the United Kingdom and Ireland through Art Data, 12 Bell Industrial Estate, 50 Cunnington Street, London W4 5HB,
tel +44 208 747 1061, fax +44 208 742 2319,
orders@artdata.co.uk

ISBN 90 5662 376 1